The Way

Using the Wisdom of Kabbalah
for Spiritual Transformation
and Fulfillment

MICHAEL BERG

JOHN WILEY & SONS, INC.

New York • Chichester • Weinheim • Brisbane • Singapore • Toronto

For more information about The Kabbalah Centre, or to learn more about our classes, books, or audio programs, please call us at 800-Kabbalah, or visit our website at www.kabbalah.com.

The Kabbalah Centre: 50 locations worldwide including New York — Los Angeles — Miami — Toronto — London — Paris — Tel Aviv

ISBN 0-471-08300-3

Printed in the United States of America

10 9 8 7 6 5 4

To Rav and Karen Berg—my teachers and my parents: I will never be able to repay you for all you have given me. You have taught me all anyone needs to know, through your words, your actions, and most importantly, through your lives. All that I am is all from you.

To my brother and friend, Yehuda: Thank you for your friendship. May we continue together to reveal this wisdom to the world.

To Monica, my wife and my love: You are so much more than any man could hope for. You are my vision of love, joy, and fulfillment. For me, you are the epitome of both physical and spiritual beauty. You are my partner and my best friend. May we complete this journey together.

To our son, David: I hope I never take for granted the great gift that you are. For me, you are pure Light.

Contents

PART ONE

The Way of Kabbalah

PART THREE

Spiritual Transformation

CHAPTER 7

Understanding Our Thoughts and Feelings   135

CHAPTER 8

Using the Spiritual Tools   149

Acknowledgments

I would like to thank the many people who have made this book possible:

Most importantly my parents and teachers, Rav and Karen Berg. One cannot hope for better parents and guides. You have taught and helped millions of people, and I am lucky to be one of them.

Rabbi Shimon bar Yochai, Rabbi Isaac Luria, Rabbi Yisrael Baal Shem Tov, Rav Yehuda Ashlag, Rav Yehuda Brandwein. This book is your wisdom. I hope I have done it justice.

Yehuda Berg, my brother, my friend, for your insights and help.

My wife, Monica, for your support, assistance, and love, and for giving me the greatest gift in our son, David.

Don Opper, Mitch Sisskind, Peter Guzzardi, and Muriel Nellis, whose help has been invaluable in bringing this book to publication.

Tom Miller, my editor at John Wiley, for his important additions and comments (which prove again that the last mile is the longest mile!).

All the people at the Kabbalah Centre, and the thousands of students who have learned with me and from me. You help me to understand these concepts better every day.

Introduction

*The wisdom of Kabbalah is a five-thousand-year-old
tradition whose purpose is to bring an end to all
pain and suffering in the world.*

Whenhen I was six years old our family was living in Jerusalem.
At that time my father and mother had made the decision not
only to devote their lives to following the spiritual teachings of
Kabbalah, but also to bring those teachings to the world.

My father, Rav Berg, had been raised in a strictly observant
Jewish environment in Brooklyn. After many years of study, he
was ordained a rabbi and spent several years teaching in a
yeshiva in New York City. But over time he grew disenchanted
with the insularity and lack of inclusiveness in the Orthodox
way of life. Eventually he began a career in business, while still
remaining observant in his personal life. After many years of
living this way, he made a trip to Israel, where he was introduced to Rabbi Yehuda Brandwein, the spiritual leader of the

Kabbalah Centre in Jerusalem and one of the twentieth century's greatest masters of the spiritual teachings of Kabbalah.
(Whenever I visit Jerusalem today and meditate on Rabbi
Brandwein's great soul, I gain wisdom and strength to live
according to kabbalistic teachings.) Through his relationship
with Rabbi Brandwein, my father made the decision to end his
business career and dedicate his life to Kabbalah. Before Rabbi
Brandwein passed on, he designated my father to succeed him
as the leader of the Kabbalah Centre.

My mother, Karen Berg, came to Kabbalah along a very different path. Her family had not been at all observant. Before
meeting my father, she led the life of a secular Jewish woman.
Yet it was she who first suggested to my father that the wisdom
of Kabbalah should be brought to humanity as a whole—that
the ancient teachings should be made available to anyone who
had a true desire to learn, regardless of their background and
religious identity, or their lack of one.

Even as small children, my brother and I were aware that this
was a truly extraordinary undertaking. Kabbalah ("to receive"
in Hebrew) is a body of mystical wisdom that had long been
kept secret from the world. Although it is really the Creator's
gift to all mankind, Kabbalah has for centuries been identified
with the esoteric or secret tradition of Judaism. Access to kabbalistic books and teachings had been granted only to scholars
whose qualifications had been established over many years, or
even over an entire lifetime.

The reasons for these prohibitions were twofold. Kabbalah
teaches that the Torah—the first five books of the Bible—was

given to Moses by the Creator. The Torah was literally dictated to Moses on Mount Sinai, as described in the Book of Exodus. Every word, every letter, of the Torah was received from God, but this was really only the beginning of the wisdom that Moses gained on Mount Sinai. The Torah, and indeed the entire Bible, is really a blueprint—an encoded introduction to a much more detailed body of wisdom that was also given to Moses by God. This was the so-called oral tradition, which was never to be written down lest it come into the possession of those who might misuse it. And even in the absence of malicious intentions, the teachings could be dangerous to those who were unprepared to receive them, in the same way that a lightning strike can overwhelm the circuitry of an ordinary household.

My parents were not only studying and living each day according to kabbalistic teachings, but were also actively making Kabbalah available to anyone who desired to learn. This was their purpose in the world. It filled every moment of their lives, and from a very early age it encompassed the lives of my brother and me as well. We adhered to all the rituals and observances given in the teachings, which Kabbalah tells us are really tools for connecting with the Light of the Creator and for fostering spiritual transformation. And we visited many spiritually important sites in Israel, including the town of Safed.

Safed was and is no ordinary place. Over the centuries Safed has been home to the greatest sages of Kabbalah. Here the mystical teachings have not only been studied but also put into practice to create a truly spiritual way of life. As my parents explained, the souls of the masters were still present in Safed, and the purpose of our visit was to connect with the souls of the kabbalistic masters who had created this extraordinary environment. Contrary to our usual understanding of death, the ancient sages had neither "departed" nor been "taken away." For them, death was not something that separated them from us in any fundamental way. It was as if they had simply gone from one room to another while remaining within the same house. Their spiritual attainments in life were so great that they were already at home in the spiritual dimension even while their bodies still lived and breathed in the physical dimension.

At the cemetery at Safed, we could still communicate directly with the great kabbalists. We could feel their presence. For us children, visiting the graves of the righteous was like entering the presence of great and wonderful people who had decided to take themselves outside the everyday world for a while. Most importantly, we could expect with absolute confidence that they would someday again be in our presence. Indeed, the resurrection of the dead and mankind's attaining immortality are basic kabbalistic teachings. As my father explained to us, these would come about through the spiritual transformation of humanity.

The night fear

One night, while I was lying in bed at the motel we were staying at in Safed, one thing worried me. For the time being, people would still have to leave this world. *They would still have to die.*

The meaning of this suddenly struck me. Someday my father and mother would no longer be physically present in my life. Someday I would have to say good-bye to them! I began to cry, rushed into my parents' room, and climbed into their bed. I kept thinking, *There has to be a way to stop this!*

There really is a way, and the purpose of this book is to tell you about it. I've called the book *The Way*—rather than *A Way, My Way,* or *One Way*—not from lack of respect for other points of view, but from a sense of responsibility to present things as I truly understand them to be. I believe that Kabbalah really is *the* way to fulfill our destiny as human beings—and that destiny is nothing less than happiness and fulfillment of an order completely different from anything else we've ever known.

Not a week goes by without my recalling that moment in the Safed motel. I really understood the limits of our lives in this world, and the importance of gaining the power to go beyond those limits. Perhaps there's been a similar moment of realization in your own life. It may have come at a time of separation and loss—at the death of a friend or relative, even of a pet. Or it may have been a less well-defined sense of something missing from your life. Like many people, you may have searched for a way to alleviate this pain. Your search may have led you to explore religious and spiritual traditions, or closely reasoned philosophies, or political causes of the left or right. It may have led you down what appear to be avenues of escape, maybe to drugs and alcohol. Eventually, like many people, you may have decided simply to accept what seemingly could not be changed, to just move on with your life, hoping that life's pain will not touch you too closely or too soon.

The benefits

This brings up the first and perhaps the most important point to be made in these pages. In my opinion, it is a mistake, though an understandable one, to lose touch with the hurt or even the rage you felt when first confronted with life's pain. That moment is an invaluable resource of energy and hunger for positive change. Whether you realize it or not, it is also a moment of real insight into the true nature of God. I believe from the bottom of my heart that the Creator did not put us into a world of pain and loss with the intention that this would be our permanent condition. Instead, we have been given the tools to fundamentally alter our destiny. We need only make a commitment to use them.

The tools are the wisdom of Kabbalah that you will find in this book. As you begin to apply these tools, I can assure you that you will see positive changes in every area of your life. It's crucial that you understand exactly what this means. Although Kabbalah has the power to ultimately end death and suffering in the world, the benefits are much more immediate. One of Kabbalah's most interesting principles relates to the *scale* of our life experiences. The greatest moments are not necessarily the obviously great ones—and we may never know which seemingly insignificant action has a far from insignificant effect on another person or even on the world. When you understand this, your whole experience of life changes. Even the most mundane tasks take on a new significance, just as fitting a small piece into a jigsaw puzzle can be more satisfying than fitting a larger, more obvious one.

Kabbalah teaches that we can bring about the end to every kind of human suffering—even death—and that we can find immense satisfaction and joy in our lives right now.

As you read on in this book and as you continue your exploration of Kabbalah beyond these pages, you will come to understand exactly what this means in your own life. For now, however, I would ask only that you read with an open mind and make a sincere effort to use what you learn in your everyday life. I think the benefits will speak for themselves.

Using this book

In order to use this book most effectively, it's best to keep a few basic ideas in mind. Remember that these opening chapters are essential, providing the foundation for everything that follows. The teachings of Kabbalah are very action-oriented, but action without understanding is incomplete. The early chapters of *The Way* are not just metaphysical theory. They are the context in which the tools of Kabbalah can be understood and most effectively put to use.

A simple analogy may clarify this. Suppose a two-year-old girl finds a plastic pencil sharpener. Having no idea what the funny little thing is for, she may assume that the sharpener is for throwing, breaking, or even eating. She has no concept of what a pencil is or how it relates to the purpose of the sharpener. Nor can she imagine the even larger purpose of writing in general, whether it's great novels or shopping lists. The girl may still "use" the sharpener, but the absence of a context makes it impossible for her to realize the true intention of the tool. *The Way* was written not only to put the tools of Kabbalah into your hands, but also to give you an understanding of how they should be employed, and the great things they can accomplish when they are used as the Creator intended. This book is not just about doing, nor is it just about understanding. It's about the inextricably interwoven nature of wisdom and action, and the ultimate purpose they share, which is the transformation of our souls.

Questions to keep in mind

1. What is the purpose of our lives?
2. What is the meaning, if any, of human pain and suffering?
3. What are the choices that lie in our power, and what is beyond our choosing?
4. How can we find peace and satisfaction in a world that often seems chaotic and dangerous?
5. How can we make a positive difference, not only for ourselves but for others as well?

PART ONE

The Way of Kabbalah

CHAPTER 1

Creating Fulfillment

Can a person's nature be changed by words on a page? Can letters and words on paper so deeply influence our consciousness that we are literally not the same person after we've read them? I believe—I *know*—that the material we are about to cover can have this effect. I have heard it over and over again, and I have discussed it and taught it on literally hundreds of occasions, and I discover something new every single time.

Let me preface this key topic with some brief observations. In recent years a number of books have tried to bring the wisdom of Kabbalah to a general audience. The great majority have been incomprehensible to most readers, and consequently they've failed to have a widespread impact. Not one of these books has discussed the concepts we will be covering in this section—which is puzzling, since they are absolutely essential kabbalistic teachings, and they're are also quite easy to understand.

Right now, before you read any further, please think for a moment about why you're looking at this page at this particular instant of your life. Are you browsing in a bookstore on your lunch hour? Perhaps you've been given *The Way* by a friend, or you're thinking of giving it as a gift yourself. Whatever the apparent reason, I would ask you to open yourself to another viewpoint—to the possibility that this is the exact moment when you are most ready to discover these teachings and take them to heart. It is said that Rabbi Isaac Luria, named the Ari, or lion, was so attuned to the state of people's souls that he could offer the precise teaching that any individual needed to hear at any given point in time. As you read this chapter, be aware that this ability on the part of the Ari was an expression of the overarching intelligence of the universe itself. There is a purpose—though perhaps a concealed one—to your reading about Kabbalah at this moment, just as there is a purpose to my writing about it. I believe from the bottom of my heart that the teachings you are about to discover can vastly—immeasurably—change your life for the better, and empower you to help others in the same way.

For each of us, life is a search. It may seem as if we're searching for different things—some for material wealth, others for knowledge, still others for fame and recognition—but these objectives are really just the outward expressions of an essential inner experience of well-being and joy. Kabbalah refers to this experience as *fulfillment,* a highly significant word.

Although many people gain brief moments of fulfillment over the course of their lives, few of us know it as an ongoing reality. It's here and then it's gone, like the flame of a match that burns for a moment and then becomes a little plume of swirling smoke. So our real search is not only for fulfillment, but for a way to somehow keep it a presence in our lives. On the very practical level of our daily experience, the purpose of Kabbalah is to make that happen—to make fulfillment a constant, not just for each individual, but for the world.

The tools of Kabbalah presented in this book don't need to be completely understood at the outset. They just need to be used. But as you use them, be sure to return again and again to the principles that underlie them, which will also be presented in these pages. These ideas should be constantly rethought. As we'll see, complacency is one of the greatest dangers to real growth. If you feel that you've thoroughly understood the concepts and that there's no need to revisit them, take it as a sign that revisiting is exactly what you need to do.

I think it's worth mentioning that I didn't make any of this up. Rather, I am privileged to have studied the wisdom of Kabbalah that has evolved over many centuries, and the purpose of *The Way* is to share that wisdom with you. There are many books on spirituality that derive from their authors' life experiences and gain their power from the authors' charisma or eloquence or depth of thought, but this is not one of those books. I do consider myself a reasonably intelligent person and an honest one, but I am not the incarnation of Kabbalah. As the person who is introducing you to this wisdom, I will try to do so to the best of my ability, but I really want you to focus on *what* I'm saying rather than *how* I'm saying it. For the few hours that you leaf through these pages, I am the medium, but the message is much larger than me. And I think you'll see just how vast that message really is as you proceed through the book.

The Creator

God is a word that frightens many people, for many different reasons.

Over the centuries, a multitude of different meanings and emotions have been attached to the word, many of them decidedly negative. The word *God* has been used to strike fear in children and to create guilt in adults. It has been used to justify military aggression and political ambition. It has come to signify a powerful and unpredictable entity that exists somewhere across a vast metaphysical divide—a being about whom it's difficult to say anything definite except that he, she, or it is very different from you or me. We've even heard fear of God described as if it were a good thing, as when someone is called a "God-fearing man."

In short, *God* is a word that carries a lot of baggage, and you may be surprised to learn that it's a word used rather sparingly in the kabbalistic teachings. One reason is the imprecise nature of the word itself. The first sentence of the Torah, for example, is usually translated, "In the beginning God created heaven and earth." A great deal has been written about this sentence, and I will have more to say about it soon, but for now let's focus on the word for *God* in the original Hebrew text. The Hebrew word is *Elohim,* which refers specifically to God's judgment—as distinct from God's mercy, or from a more all-inclusive sense of God as an omniscient presence. In general, Kabbalah refers to God as the Creator, or as *ein sof,* which can loosely be translated as "the infinite."

In keeping with this preference, we'll rarely use the word *God* in this book, and most often we'll speak of the Creator. Although we will occasionally use the personal pronoun "He" when referring to the Creator, this is only for the sake of grammatical efficiency. Kabbalah teaches that a distinction does exist between male and female energies, but that the Creator transcends these gender categories. "He" encompasses both forms of energy. The Creator is an infinite force of positive energy, without beginning or end; the essence of all hope, peace, contentment, mercy, and fulfillment; the source of everything in Creation that opposes the forces of confusion and chaos and suffering and pain; an endless source of Light; and an unnamable timeless presence.

But these are attributes of the Creator, in the same way that judgment and mercy are attributes. They are the Creator's *creations*—but the whole of the Creator is unknowable and beyond our comprehension.

The energy of the Creator is carefully and lovingly distributed in our world, because the Creator's deepest intention is to share with us peace, joy, kindness, and love.

Kabbalah teaches that this sharing permeates the natural world—in physical things such as apples and airplanes, as well as in intangibles such as affection, loyalty, and kindness. Through these and all the other infinite varieties of matter and feeling, we catch a tiny glimpse—and only a glimpse—of the Creator's nature.

The Light of the Creator

Kabbalah refers to all these manifestations as *the Light of the Creator*. The Light is not only knowable, it is something we encounter in one form or another virtually every day. When we look into the eyes of children and are overwhelmed by their innocence and perfection, this is an aspect of the Light of the Creator. When we take pride in a job well done, when we treat others with respect, when we marvel at natural beauty or at a beautifully realized work of art, we are encountering the Light; conversely, sadness, loss of hope, and negativity in our lives are expressions of our separation from the Light. Kabbalah tells us that the feelings of peace, joy, and understanding that we gain from experiences of the Light in the physical realm only hint at the infinite fulfillment that is the Creator's essence. And whether we realize it or not, it is union with this essence that we're all searching for.

Unfortunately, the real meaning of this union and of the fulfillment that it brings are difficult concepts for most people to understand. Very often they're misconstrued as money, fame, power, or other tangible and temporary attributes of everyday life. Many of us are searching for those things, and we take pleasure in the excitement and satisfaction that they bring. But what if there were a way to make fulfillment a permanent presence, not just in your own life, but for literally everyone in the world?

The principles of Kabbalah introduced in this book guarantee that fulfillment. They just need to be used, and they can be used even before they're fully understood. Intellectual understanding is not the ultimate goal. Thinking about the concepts—and especially putting them into action in the real world—are what counts.

Kabbalah gives us the tools to stay connected to the Creator's Light, and we accomplish this by drawing out the Light that is already within us.

We don't have to reach out to acquire anything new. We only need to take control of the power that has already been given to us. In fact, this power, the Light of the Creator, is the very stuff of which we are made—and deep down, we *know* this to be true. We feel that there's something transcendent within us, if only we could somehow make contact with it.

Much research has demonstrated that the overwhelming majority of us believe in some form of higher power, and many believe in God in a very traditional sense: God is all-powerful, and God is good. But how can an omnipotent, benevolent God allow the obvious pain and suffering that afflict our world to come into being, much less continue and even intensify? Is it naive to declare that this just doesn't make any sense? According to Kabbalah, it's not in the least naive. It's a major realization, and it's also the first step toward understanding what the Creator really intended. By revealing the Light of the

Creator in ourselves and in the world around us, we can at last realize that intention. We can bring peace, joy, and fulfillment to all mankind.

The rocky path to transformation

Not long ago a student at the Kabbalah Centre in Los Angeles adopted a baby from China. Lori was nine months old at the time of her adoption, but her physical development was that of a child at least four months younger. She had spent almost her whole life lying flat on her back in an orphanage crib. She could not sit up or even roll over by herself. The back of her head had actually begun to flatten out due to her lack of mobility, and there was a large bald spot where her hair had been unable to grow.

When she arrived in America, for the first time Lori had a chance to move around on her own. Following the instructions of their pediatrician, her parents put a blanket on the floor and gently placed Lori in the center of it. At first she was so terrified that she seemed to enter a sort of trancelike state in order to escape the new and completely disorienting situation in which she found herself. And if any attempt was made to turn her over or stimulate her, she cried bitterly and quickly returned to her "comfort zone" on her back. To her parents, Lori seemed to be making no progress at all—yet Lori's doctor was surprisingly confident. There was no evidence of underlying neuromuscular damage, and, as the doctor put it, "Lori will eventually learn to walk because that's what she is meant to do. She's also meant to experience difficulty in walking, so that by overcoming those difficulties she can become stronger."

Before long, day by day, Lori began to make progress, though at first even the smallest transitions seemed terribly painful. If she managed to turn over, she immediately cried out in pain and again rolled onto her back. But later—sometimes after an hour, and sometimes after a full day—she would try again. Gradually progress happened more quickly, and within six months what had once seemed impossible had become reality. Lori had caught up. She could do everything that was to be expected of a child her age.

Why did Lori not simply give up when her first attempts at growth were so painful? Why did she not behave in accordance with a behaviorist model of pain avoidance? Why did this child, in her small way, choose to transform herself from one mode of existence to another? The answer, as her doctor pointed out, is that it was in her nature to do so. The difficulties she experienced, however painful they may have seemed, were simply of a different order of magnitude than the deeply ingrained objective of learning to walk.

On the path to transformation, you will undergo exactly this sort of experience. The path includes many obstacles, but the obstacles themselves are opportunities to renew your journey toward joy and fulfillment. It's misleading to speak of Kabbalah as difficult or demanding, because that places emphasis in the wrong place. *Again, the obstacles are of a different order of magnitude than the objective.* When you learned to walk, to speak, to read, or even to ride a bicycle, there were certainly mistakes and scraped knees and perhaps even a broken bone or two, but it was in your nature to accept and even to seek out those experiences as the price of positive change and ultimate fulfillment.

This—not sorrow, pain, or death—is your true destiny. But you are not just a recipient of this fulfillment. The Creator intends for you to be an essential participant in bringing it about, using the spiritual tools of Kabbalah that have been given to all mankind.

The Way is a user's manual for those tools. But it is not a quick fix. As we've discussed, transformation is not easy, nor is it supposed to be easy.

A kabbalistic tale makes this point very clearly.

Accomplish what you came here for

There was once a great scholar named Rabbi Naftali Zvi Yehuda Berlin, who had become known as the Netziv. He had many students and he had written dozens of books. One day the Netziv spoke to his students about how he had chosen his life's path, and this is the story he told:

When I was ten years old, I was a poor student. When I went to class, I fooled around. I didn't listen to my teachers. I was in trouble all the time. And one day I was in my room and I heard my mother crying as she talked with my father. I sneaked up to their bedroom door and listened. My mother said, "What are we going to do with Naftali? He doesn't study. He's failing his classes. They don't want to allow him back in school. Without schooling, he'll never amount to anything." I was shocked. I felt terrible that I had brought so much anguish to my mother. I dragged myself back to my room and I made a decision—from that day on I would focus on my studies and stop fooling around and listen to my teachers so that my mother would be happy again. And as you can see, I continued my studies, and I became a scholar, and now I'm a teacher with thousands of students and I've written many books.

But I often wonder what would have happened if I didn't hear my mother crying that day. I'm certain that I would have grown up to be a very nice person. I would have been the kind of person who gave to charity and went to synagogue regularly and prayed and studied a little and took care of my family in the best way that I knew. I would have lived a good, simple life. And after so many years I would die and stand before the Creator and the Creator would say, "Well, Rabbi Naftali."

Rabbi? What is He saying? I'm not a rabbi. I'm a nice guy, I'm a nice person, but I'm not a rabbi. Maybe there's been a mistake. But before I could correct Him, He would say, "Where are all your students?"

Students? Is He crazy? Where would I get students? I'm a simple guy. I'm a nice guy, but what do I know about teaching? I barely finished school. He's got me mixed up with somebody else. But before I could set Him straight, the Creator would ask, "And where are all the books that you've written?"

Books? What books? I could hardly read, let alone write. I could read the prayers. But books? No, I hadn't written any books.

And the Creator would have been disappointed.

Why? Why disappointed? I would have been a good person. A simple man, it's true, but good. I wouldn't have written any books, but I would have done no evil in the world. I wouldn't have any students, it's true, but hadn't I taken care of my family? Hadn't I given to charity and gone to synagogue regularly and learned all the prayers? Isn't that enough? What right would the Creator have to be disappointed in me?

The Creator would have a right to be disappointed because had I not heard my mother that day, I would not have reached my potential. Living a good, simple life—even a spiritual life—was not enough. Because the fact is all of us are put into this world with a particular job to do. Just because a person lives a good life doesn't mean that he accomplished what he was put into this world to do. And if we don't accomplish what we were put here to do, we disappoint the Creator, and we've wasted our lives.

But, you ask, how are we to know? How can we understand what we were put into this world to do? We are simple people. We can't see into the future. We can't know what the Creator has in mind for us.

And, of course, that's true. So the only way we can hope to achieve what we came into this world to accomplish, the only way we can hope to satisfy the Creator, is to always push ourselves to the limits of our potential and to never be satisfied with our spiritual accomplishments. Our job in this world is not about being a good person, or a spiritual person, or a wise person. It's not about giving a little charity or being nice to people and attending synagogue. It's about doing what we came to the world to accomplish. And though we may *not* know *exactly* what we came here for, we *do* know that without a constant push to change for the better, without our constant endeavor toward spiritual growth, we can never hope to fulfill our potential. And this is what the Creator expects of us.

This tale reveals a basic distinction between Kabbalah and other spiritual teachings. Kabbalah emphasizes that obstacles and challenges are guideposts to our true purpose in the world. They are stepping-stones to genuine transformation for each of us as individuals, and through us, for humanity as a whole. To understand exactly what this means, it's best to begin at the beginning, with Kabbalah's teaching of how the universe was created.

As we'll see in the next chapter, creation is not an event that took place at some distant point in the past. It is a continuing endeavor in which we participate at every moment, and the purpose of this book is to help you take part in that process in a way that brings you peace, joy, and ultimate fulfillment.

CHAPTER 2

Kabbalah through the Ages

According to kabbalistic teaching, the wisdom of Kabbalah existed even before the physical universe came into being. As the process of creation took place, the wisdom was given by the Creator to Adam in the Garden of Eden, which really was paradise—or would have been paradise if the process of creation had been completed and Adam and Eve had not sinned. Concerning the sin, Kabbalah describes what took place in great detail, from both the physical and the spiritual perspective. For example, when Adam and Eve were banished from the Garden, the Creator told them, *"Because you ate of the tree about which I commanded you, 'You shall not eat of it,' cursed be the ground because of you; by toil shall you eat of it all the days of your life."*

On the one hand, Kabbalah tells us that this refers to an

actual event in human history: Adam and Eve were real people who did eat a fruit from a forbidden tree. At the same time, it is an allegory of humanity's descent from a spiritual state of being to mortal life in the physical world. When the Creator tells Adam that he must till the soil, Kabbalah understands this to mean that we must immerse ourselves in the physical world. We must take tangible action to ensure survival and prosperity, not only of our bodies, but of our souls as well.

Abraham created a portal

The opening books of the Bible describe how the spiritual system of Kabbalah was brought into being following the expulsion from the Garden of Eden. This concept of a spiritual system is fundamental, but it doesn't refer to any sort of physical circuitry. Rather, in the process of living their own lives, the biblical patriarchs and matriarchs made themselves the conduits through which we can draw closer to the Creator and form a connection with His wisdom and His love.

Kabbalists speak of the patriarch Abraham as "opening" the qualities of mercy and kindness. He created a portal, like an open telephone line, which allows us to connect with divine wisdom.

To a kabbalist, then, Abraham, Isaac Jacob, Rachel, and Leah are not literary characters. They were real people whose lives are chronicled in the Bible because of their spiritual accomplishments, because they represent qualities and characteristics to which we can all aspire, and because they created the means whereby we can gain ultimate fulfullment. Indeed, they are still available to us as resources of spiritual energy for dealing with the challenges and obstacles of our lives.

Through prayer, meditation, and simply by living in accordance with kabbalistic principles, we can maintain an open line of communication with the spiritual dimension of reality that the kabbalists refer to as the Upper Worlds.

While this is not necessarily an easy concept to grasp, it's an extremely vital one. Its meaning will become clearer as you read this book and as you explore the great kabbalistic teachings of the past.

The powers of the letters

The first kabbalistic text was a small book entitled *Sefer Yetzirah* —in English, *The Book of Formation*—composed by Abraham the Patriarch approximately four thousand years ago. *The Book of Formation* presents a detailed explication of the mystical powers of the Hebrew alphabet, whose letters were employed by the Creator in many different combinations to create the physical universe. In the same way that modern science refers to atoms as the energy building blocks of physical reality, *The Book of Formation* describes the Hebrew letters as the foundation of the sun, moon, and stars. Even intangibles such as love, mercy, and time derive from the twenty-two letters of the Hebrew alphabet. Each letter has a specific energy, and each reveals a particular aspect of the Creator.

חזוהדגבא

סנמלכיט

תשרקצפע

The letters are seen here as they appear in a painstakingly handwritten Torah scroll. Kabbalistically, this is the authentic form of the alphabet. Close inspection reveals that many of the letters build on the designs of those that came earlier. In Hebrew, the language itself is referred to as *evrit*, a derivative of the verb *lavir*, meaning "to transfer" or "to carry over," and the letters are the medium through which divine energy passes into the physical world.

Kabbalah teaches that the letters are much more than visual symbols corresponding to specific sounds. Like the atomic elements of the periodic table, they are the fundamental configurations of energy that make up the world. The properties and powers of each letter are as different as hydrogen from uranium, and each has its specific benefit and use. Vocalizing the letters, or even just looking at them, creates a resonance at the deepest levels of our being.

A powerful series of three-letter sequences known as the 72 Names of God has been used for centuries to connect to specific manifestations of positive energy, including health, prosperity, certainty, and many others. The Hebrew letters are a very rich subject. They have deservedly been the subject of a number of books. As you move forward in the study of Kabbalah, your understanding and respect for the powers of the letters is sure to increase.

The *Zohar*

Kabbalah's most important book is the *Zohar,* or *Book of Splendor.* It was composed in Aramaic two thousand years ago by Rabbi Shimon bar Yochai. Rabbi Shimon is said to have received the text from Moses himself, just as Moses received the Law directly from the Creator. Over thousands of pages, the Zohar presents dialogues between masters and students concerning incidents in the Bible and other spiritual subjects.

The structure of the Zohar is supremely diffuse and elusive. Topics opened at one point may disappear for long stretches before they reappear. Perhaps because of the difficulty of the text and the powers said to reside in it, access to the Zohar was often severely restricted. For centuries only married male scholars over the age of forty were authorized to read the Zohar. Now the entire Zohar has been translated into English by the Kabbalah Centre, and the Light that resides in this sacred text is available to everyone.

A turning point in the history of Kabbalah took place at the end of the fifteenth century. With the rise of a fanatical Catholicism in the Iberian Peninsula, an edict of King Ferdinand and Queen Isabella expelled all Jews from Spain in 1492. Although they had achieved power and influence in Spanish society over many generations, Jews now found themselves in exile yet again, as they had many times in the biblical era. This experience, and the challenge of interpreting it, is basic to the developments in Kabbalah during the next hundred years—and in particular to the work of the great kabbalist Rabbi Isaac Luria.

Rabbi Luria and *tikkun*

Born in Jerusalem in 1534, Rabbi Luria lived at a time when Jewish life had been fundamentally destabilized by the Spanish expulsion and the sense of fragmentation and loss that accompanied it. He began spiritual studies while in his twenties. After years in seclusion studying the Zohar, a vision of the prophet Elijah instructed him to move to the town of Safed in Galilee, where an intensely spiritual community had grown up around the kabbalists Rabbi Moses Cordovero and Rabbi Joseph Karo. Here kabbalistic precepts were not only studied but were put into proactive practice in all areas of life. Rabbi Cordovero's *Thirteen Principles* included admonitions to love all beings, even those who torment us; to share everything we have; and to refrain from judgment under all circumstances.

In Safed, Rabbi Luria was quickly recognized as a spiritual master and assumed leadership of a group of students known as the Cubs, in deference to Rabbi Luria's own designation as the Ari, or Lion. Although Rabbi Luria wrote nothing himself, his teachings were transcribed by the kabbalist Rabbi Chaim Vital. Rabbi Luria lived for only three years after his arrival in

Safed, but his ideas are a fundamental element in the wisdom of Kabbalah and in the spiritual heritage of all mankind.

Specifically, Rabbi Luria provided a new perspective on the Zohar by organizing topics covered in diverse parts of the text. He also developed the concept of *tikkun*—usually translated as *correction* or *repair*—which deals with the purpose of life, the presence of pain and suffering, and the ultimate transformation of all humanity.

Opening to the Light

A general theme in the history of Kabbalah is its progression from inaccessibility and suppression toward availability to humanity as a whole. Rabbi Luria's work in systematizing the content of the Zohar was a step in this direction. A further step was taken almost two hundred years later by Israel ben Eliezer (1700–1760, also known as the Baal Shem Tov, or Master of the Good Name).

Living in Central Europe at a time when Torah studies were dominated by intricate scholarship and complex reasoning, the Baal Shem Tov rekindled a highly emotional, intuitive relationship with the Creator. His personal history reads like a story from the Zohar, in which humble beggars and artisans suddenly turn out to be enlightened sages. Certainly he was very different from Rabbi Luria, who was recognized from the first as a brilliant intellect. During the first part of his life, the Baal Shem was thought to be a good-hearted but ignorant fool. He did menial tasks in the synagogue of his hometown in southern

Poland. Then one day, to everyone's amazement, a highly respected rabbi suddenly announced his intention of becoming the disciple of the humble synagogue handyman. Needless to say, this caused quite a sensation. The Baal Shem Tov soon had a large group of students, as well as adversaries who felt he was vulgarizing the sacred teachings. In contrast to the complex mystical discourses of Rabbi Luria and the other Safed kabbalists, the Baal Shem Tov presented his teachings through stories and parables of simple elegance. By so doing, he made Kabbalah accessible to anyone who chose to listen and learn. Throughout this book we will rely heavily on the tales of the Baal Shem Tov.

Rabbi Yehuda Ashlag (1886–1955) continued along the same path. Among his many writings is a translation of the entire Zohar from Aramaic to modern Hebrew, together with a detailed commentary on the text. Rabbi Ashlag was born in Europe but lived most of his adult life in Jerusalem, where he founded the Kabbalah Centre in 1922. His work was continued by his student Rabbi Yehuda Brandwein (1903–1969) and was ultimately brought to fruition by my parents, Rav Berg and Karen Berg, under whose leadership Kabbalah Centres have been established throughout the world. The purpose of these Centres is not only to bring the wisdom of Kabbalah to all who have a desire to learn, but also to put this wisdom into practice in every area of life.

The history of Kabbalah is a gradual revelation of knowledge to an ever-expanding base of people. What started as a tradition of knowledge passed "from lip to ear" has blossomed into a movement to bring the knowledge to ordinary people all over the world. This is by no means an accident or coincidence. As we'll discuss in the chapters that follow, the ever-widening dissemination of Kabbalah's wisdom is part of a process that has been going on literally since time began.

Advanced Kabbalah

New Kabbalah students are often well educated and possessed of inquiring minds. For them, the intellectual element of Kabbalah can be very appealing. It's well known that many great thinkers have explored this tradition, and the similarities between kabbalistic ideas and cutting-edge science also quickly become apparent. As they open the Zohar for the first time, students may feel that they're stepping into an alternate universe of arcane knowledge. Complications, paradoxes, and even perceived difficulties can be part of the attraction.

It's true that kabbalistic study can be intellectually challenging, but Kabbalah is not higher mathematics. It is not just an internally consistent, self-referential system whose very intricacy is its justification for being. Highly intelligent people like to use their minds just as great athletes like to exercise their bodies, but to understand Kabbalah, we must take care that this does not become an end in itself

The dangers of this are evident in much of the Kabbalah material that's currently in the marketplace. Most books on the topic are highly inaccessible, if not altogether impossible to understand. Part of the reason for this is an urge toward intellectual tap dancing that seems to afflict writers on this topic, particularly those who have recently discovered Kabbalah.

This is not to say that thoughtful secular authorities are unfamiliar with the teachings. Gershom Scholem, for example, was immensely knowledgeable about the tradition from a scholarly perspective. But after reading only a few pages of an academic book on Kabbalah, we may well find ourselves in a maze of discourse on the *sefirot*, the *Shekinah*, and the *Shulchan Arukh*. This is kabbalistic knowledge, but not kabbalistic wisdom. In fact, such wanderings can lead a reader away from rather than toward the wisdom of the Creator. This wisdom, the sages tell us, is the power to "see the end in the beginning," to recognize the full-grown tree in the newly planted seed, and, most importantly, to express that vision as action in the physical world.

At the Kabbalah Centre, we present Kabbalah as a deeply spiritual but *practical* system for improving your life in all areas —with the added understanding that your personal transformation will hasten the unity of all mankind with God. Our intention is to make Kabbalah accessible, not inscrutable, especially since the latter option has been the choice of so many authors.

At the same time, I recognize that Kabbalah is meant to engage the mind as well as the heart. Those who discover new analogies, hidden parallels, and subtle interpretations of the Zohar surely bring joy to the Creator. But without in any way advocating a narrow anti-intellectualism in *The Way*'s presentation of Kabbalah, I would invoke Shakespeare's observation that simple truth is often miscalled simplicity. Kabbalah must never be cast as an intellectual conundrum. Thought must always be linked to feeling, and feeling to positive action right now, wherever you are and whomever you're with.

The following story has been told many times, but it's so powerful and enlightening that it bears repeating once again, In fact, no book on Kabbalah would be complete without it.

During the time of the Roman Empire, the great sage Hillel was asked by a student if he could teach the entire wisdom of the universe while standing on one foot. It is not recorded which foot he chose to stand on, but what Hillel said has come down to us through the ages. "Love thy neighbor as thyself," he told the student. "The rest is only commentary."

There are many commentaries, but with all due respect, I don't want this book to be another one. "Love thy neighbor" is the secret of living in accordance with Kabbalah, and it is the message of *The Way* as well.

CHAPTER 3

The Light and
the Vessel

All cultures have creation stories, most of which are largely unchanged beyond the reach of memory. This is not the case with Kabbalah's view of creation, which has continued to develop and evolve. Certain elements of the material we are about to cover are very old, but great insights have appeared even within the last hundred years. The Zohar, for example, was composed almost two thousand years ago—but its narrative of creation cannot be completely understood without Rabbi Ashlag's commentary in *The Ten Luminous Emanations,* written in the 1930s.

The ongoing nature of Kabbalah's creation story is very much in keeping with the content of the story itself.

Kabbalah teaches that the universe is not a "finished product," and that its construction is in progress even at this very moment. We are all building it, in partnership with the Creator.

The world, therefore, is not something that just happens to us. *It is something that we make happen.* Right now, whether you realize it or not, you are building the environment that determines every aspect of your life. And as with any construction project, it's much easier with the proper tools than without them. That's why the spiritual tools of Kabbalah are so absolutely necessary.

In this chapter we will consider the creation story from three perspectives:

1. First, as a metaphysical process that describes and explains the existence of the physical world.

2. Then as an expression of the historical experience of mankind as a whole.

3. And finally, as a paradigm of the individual inner journey that every soul travels over the course of a lifetime.

Light and Vessel: The metaphysics of creation

At the start of the second millennium, the life span of a typical person is something over seventy years, or roughly thirty thousand days. While we may not like to admit it, most of those days are not particularly memorable ones. Days, weeks, and even months can run together in a routine—until something comes along that's really out of the ordinary, something that makes a certain day or a certain instant stand out forever in our memory. It may be a moment of personal crisis, such as an accident or a family emergency. Or it may be an occasion of unforgettable happiness.

Right now, if you were to search your memory for the most overwhelmingly joyful times of your life, what would you come up with? For many people, it's the birth of a child or a family celebration, such as a graduation or a wedding. The details can certainly vary, and I have no way of knowing the specifics of your life's happiest times, but from a kabbalistic perspective I can make some rather confident statements about them.

First, however it may have seemed to you at the time, the real source of your joy lay outside the realm of tangible objects or physical sensations. These were central to the experience only because they ignited a very special kind of spark somewhere deep in your consciousness. If you made a last-second winning shot in a basketball game, it wasn't the optical process of seeing the ball go through the net that made you so happy. After all, the players on the opposing team saw the same thing, and it didn't bring them any joy. The truth is, the most wonderful moments of our lives—Kabbalah calls them moments of fulfillment—have physical antecedents, but they're really experiences that take place within our hearts and souls.

My second observation about the happiest times of your life is actually a powerful kabbalistic lesson. Kabbalah tells us that our moments of greatest joy take place for a very specific reason: they are intended to give us just the tiniest glimpse of what real joy is like. They are microscopic windows into the real experience of spiritual fulfillment.

So if the most wonderful moments of your life were only a fraction of true fulfillment, you'd no doubt like to know how to get to the real thing. How to get as much fulfillment as possible. How to experience *every minute of every day* at an exponentially higher level of joy than anything you've ever known.

Is such a thing really possible? Well, yes—but in order to understand how, we have to take a step back. Quite a big step, in fact, to before the dawn of creation itself.

The Light

The Bible begins with the famous phrase "In the beginning," but Kabbalah tells us that a great deal preceded the beginning. Before the creation of time and space, there existed an infinite positive energy—the source of all that "is," "was," and "will be." Since there was no space in the sense that we now understand the word, it would be misleading to say that the energy was everywhere. But we can say that there was *nowhere that it was not.*

The Hebrew word for this energy is *Or,* which can be translated as Light. But the Light of the Creator is far more than anything we might associate with an electric lightbulb, a flash of lightning, or any form of light in the physical world.

In kabbalistic terms, Light is a code word for an all-encompassing radiance of divine love.

Just as sunlight includes every color of the spectrum, the Light of the Creator includes all that we truly want and need—

not only tangible things, but also emotional and spiritual qualities such as love, happiness, trust, and beauty. Just as it's impossible to describe the Creator, the Light is a source of complete and permanent fulfillment that can't really be expressed in words. This is the Light of fulfillment that you've just barely glimpsed at the most joyful moments of your life.

Of all the attributes of the Creator that are encompassed by the Light, the essential and defining one is an infinite and unbounded desire to give and share of itself.

The desire to share is both the fundamental attribute of the Creator and the true reason for the creation of the universe. As the great kabbalist Rabbi Moshe Chaim Luzzatto (1707–1747) wrote in *The Way of God,* "The purpose of creation was to bring into being a creature who could derive pleasure from the goodness of God." What an amazing statement this is. It means that everything came into being in order for us to enjoy it. So many wars, persecutions, and general human miseries have been perpetrated over the centuries, supposedly because they were the will of God. Yet Kabbalah tells us that God's will is for us to find pleasure in His creation! That's literally why we're here. The Creator's desire to share was the true impetus for the process of creation.

The Vessel

The Creator's desire to share implied the creation of something to *share with:* a receiving entity to accept the Light. Kabbalah refers to this receiving entity as the *Vessel*. Kabbalistic teachings emphasize that because the Light was everywhere, the Vessel was formed of this sharing energy, but with a new energy of *receiving* that was not only the first but also the only *ex nihilo* true creation that has ever taken place. The Vessel, in other words, incorporated a new essence that was the reciprocal of the Creator's giving nature. By the will of the Creator, the Vessel came instantly into being. There is no time lag between the Creator's intentions and the realization of those intentions. In fact, the primordial events we're now speaking of took place before time and space had even come into existence.

The shattering

The dual nature of the Vessel—formed of the Light, but with an essence of receiving—was a basic duality that amplified itself as the process of creation continued. As the Vessel continued to receive the Light, its receiving energy sought unity with the Light's sharing essence. It was as if a glass were being filled with a warm liquid: gradually the temperature of the glass itself begins to rise, to match the essential characteristic of the substance it's receiving. If we can ascribe human characteristics to the Vessel for a moment, we could say that it wanted to express the qualities of the Creator. It wanted to be more like the Creator. It even wanted to *become one* with the all-giving Creator. But it could not achieve this as long as it could only receive and never give.

So the Vessel pushed back against the Light and the Light

withdrew. In Hebrew this event is called the *tsimtsum,* which has connotations of both restriction and constriction. As the Light and the Vessel separated, the Vessel became a point of utter darkness—and the effect was like a vacuum that demands to be filled. In an instant the Vessel experienced an indescribable sense of withdrawal from the Creator's nurturing Light. Having wanted the Light to withdraw, the Vessel now desperately wanted it back. And the Light did return. It rushed back into the Vessel at full force.

But the duality within the Vessel still remained: the unresolved paradox of its essential nature of receiving and its desire to take on the giving nature of the Creator. And the effect of this duality was intensified by the Light's sudden and overwhelming reappearance. The Vessel had desired the return of the Light, but it wasn't really prepared to accept that return. In one immeasurably small moment the Vessel took the full force of the returning Light, and the result was the defining event of all kabbalistic teaching. At that instant, the Vessel shattered. It exploded into an infinite number of fragments, which became our universe.

A fascinating aspect of Kabbalah is the extent to which the shattering of the Vessel corresponds to the Big Bang theory of creation, which is now almost universally accepted by modern science. According to this theory, the universe came into being when an infinitely dense entity, currently thought to have been about the size of a dime, exploded outward with inconceivable force. This seems fairly straightforward, but it's a much more complicated idea than it appears. We're inclined to think, for example, of the primordial dime-sized entity as exploding into space—but there was no space before the explosion. Space exploded, and time exploded from the entity along with matter. While matter is tangible, and space and time are not, all three came into being at once. All three are remnants of the Big Bang. This is a key realization, because it allows us to see that our consciousness derives from the shattered Vessel along with our physical selves. Like space and time, consciousness cannot be seen or touched, but Kabbalah teaches that it contains the same essential elements as our bodies or the chair across the room. It is the product of the interaction between the Light and the Vessel, and of the duality of giving and receiving that caused the Vessel to shatter.

What an extraordinary event the kabbalists described here! It's the transformation of spiritual energy into material reality, but this is only the beginning. Remember: the Vessel aspired to Oneness with the Creator. Its intention was to transform its essence from receiving for itself alone to absolutely selfless giving and sharing. The process began at the instant of restriction, when the Vessel "pushed back" and stopped receiving the Light.

And the process is continuing at this moment—because the intention of the Vessel was not fulfilled, and we are fragments of the Vessel in the physical world.

Again, every aspect of our being continues to express the Vessel's struggle to resolve its dual nature. Every cell embodies this paradox. Every action is an expression of it. Every thought and every feeling reflect it.

Reconnecting with the Light

So what's the solution? How can we resolve this inner duality? How can we change our fundamentally conflicted experience of life into the pure fulfillment that we discussed at the start of this chapter? In a word, the answer is *transformation*—but what does this really mean? Please read the next few sentences very carefully, because the rest of this book will be useful only if these ideas are thoroughly understood.

Kabbalah teaches that transformation means becoming a being of giving and sharing. This refers to more than acts of sharing. It means connecting with the Light, becoming one with the Creator, and making your essence and the essence of the Creator one and the same.

And how is that done? Simply put, it's done by using the tools and teachings of Kabbalah presented in these pages, always interwoven with a heartfelt intention to become a truly sharing being, to achieve oneness with the Creator.

These ideas, I deeply believe, present a whole new paradigm for how to live our lives. Our entire society is based on the idea that *getting* is the foundation of happiness. It's a message we take in hundreds of times every day: *get* a larger income, *get* a good education, *get* the best mortgage rate, *get* the feeling that you're loved, valued, and appreciated at home and at work. But Kabbalah tells us that this is an illusion. What we really want and need is neither more material goods nor more excitement nor greater sensual pleasure. There's no reason to be scornful of those things, but they're superficial compared to our deepest and most authentic desire, which is for the fulfillment that comes from connection with the Light.

But just as it is in our power to connect to the Light, we can also disconnect. Just as we can achieve oneness with the Creator, we can also estrange ourselves from Him. Just as giving and sharing are the essence of the Creator's nature and the source of all that is good in the world, all chaos, pain, suffering, and even death likewise have a common origin. According to kabbalistic teaching, the origin of all negativity is the *desire to receive for ourselves alone.* This self-serving desire, in any of its countless forms, cuts us off from the Light, distances us from the Creator, and makes true fulfillment impossible. To the extent we are connected to this desire, we are disconnected from the essence of the Creator.

Yet the desire to receive for ourselves alone is inherent in our nature as human beings. The human body itself is a pure expression of it! Although from time to time people have walked the earth who had the capacity to completely transcend the parameters of the human condition, most of us are not able to extinguish desire per se from our daily experience, nor does Kabbalah urge us to extinguish it.

Kabbalah teaches us and empowers us to integrate the dual aspects of our being that are our legacy from the primordial Vessel by transforming desire to receive for ourselves alone into desire to receive for the purpose of sharing.

These ideas may at first seem complex, but they express themselves in very tangible ways every day. For now, in order to clarify the crucial distinction between receiving for oneself and receiving in order to share, think again of water being poured into a glass. If the water keeps coming, the glass will eventually overflow. It might even shatter if the force of the water is strong enough. But if the glass is connected to other glasses, if all that it receives is shared rather than retained, a circuitry is created that fulfills the needs of all the components.

By translating the metaphor of the glass into our lives in the real world, we achieve oneness with the sharing nature of the Creator, and the Creator's intention of infinite giving to us is also fulfilled.

The four central principles of the Way

1. Our deepest desire and need is for the fulfillment that comes from oneness with the Creator. This is what we're really seeking when we experience pleasure in any form.

2. True fulfillment, Kabbalah tells us, comes with *transformation:* that is, from connection with the Light of the Creator, from making our nature and His nature of sharing and giving one and the same.

3. Most importantly, achieving transformation means becoming a *being of sharing.* Notice that this refers to an inner condition rather than any physical action or activity. It means using the tools and teachings of Kabbalah with the sincere intention to transform.

4. Desire to receive for ourselves alone cuts us off from the Light of the Creator and makes true fulfillment impossible. Yet self-serving desire is built into our condition as human

beings. The answer lies not in ridding ourselves of all desire, but in transforming self-serving *desire into desire to receive for the purpose of sharing.*

Our own best interests

In presenting these ideas to new students of Kabbalah, I've noticed several very common responses. Many people are struck by what they perceive as the nobility of the idea of receiving in order to share—and as a corollary to this, people sometimes feel they ought to immediately start a "holy" life, which might include giving away all their possessions or some other equivalent of sleeping on a bed of nails. Both these reactions are well-intentioned, but mistaken. First, Kabbalah is not really about altruism, charity, or even nobility in the sense that these words are usually understood.

Spiritual transformation is in our own interest, and we should undertake it for our own good.

It's true that by changing ourselves we foster positive change in others, but this, too, is ultimately for our own benefit. Kabbalah teaches that when a sufficient number of people have achieved transformation, a kind of critical mass will be reached and the redemption of the world will be achieved. We will at last complete the process of creation that was begun in the Garden of Eden, that was diverted by the sin of Adam, and that has been the goal of humanity ever since. We will have regained the freedom from pain, suffering, and death that was intended for us by the Creator. In Kabbalistic terms, this is what the coming of the Messiah really means—and what could be more in our own interests than that?

The precipitous impulse to "start sharing like mad" requires a bit more explanation. For new students of Kabbalah, it's safe to say that transformation should be more about inner growth than external action. Once again, the basis of transformation is becoming a *being of sharing*. Until we achieve this, anything we do in the physical world will be more or less irrelevant from a spiritual point of view. On the other hand, once we do accomplish our inner work, *all* our actions will be expressions of our connection to the Light.

Remember: the primordial Vessel shattered when it received more Light than it was constituted to receive.

A principle of Kabbalah states: *There can be no coercion in spirituality.* No one, not even the Creator, can impose the Light upon a Vessel that is not prepared to receive it. Conversely, the Light is always there for us once we *are* prepared.

We must prepare our inner selves—using sharing, study, prayer, and the other tools of Kabbalah—so that our physical actions are congruent with the state of our souls.

The intention of sharing

Everything we do in the world—whether it's studying the sacred texts or working to help the poor—must be infused with a yearning for transformation and fulfillment. This is what defines a truly spiritual person, and this is the measure by which his or her actions should be understood.

Suppose a famous surgeon attended a piano recital and was deeply moved. The next day he decided to try playing the piano himself. He discovered he enjoyed it, and he suspected that he might even have a talent for it. He contacted a piano teacher and scheduled a lesson. At the end of the lesson the teacher complimented the surgeon and told him that it might indeed be worthwhile for him to study the piano. Excited and inspired by this, the surgeon scheduled several more lessons.

All this is very positive—playing the piano is a good thing—but suppose his new interest begins to distract the surgeon from his practice? If he reduces the number of patients he sees in order to attend his piano lessons, he's sacrificed his greatest gift for a less significant one. He's cut back on his life's work of helping others in order to do something that, for him at least, is more of a simple entertainment.

There's nothing wrong with striving for self-improvement, but Kabbalah teaches that the highest level of striving is for transformation—for turning the desire to receive for ourselves alone into the desire to receive for the purpose of sharing.

Any action that is performed with this intention is an act of merit. Without this intention, even "good deeds" lack the defining element.

Please be aware that these principles are an absolutely essential foundation for understanding the rest of this book, for using the tools of Kabbalah that it presents, and for achieving the connection with the Light that is our true purpose in life. It might be helpful to look over this chapter again before reading further. Explaining the ideas to a friend or family member in your own words can also help clarify your own understanding. Or you might try writing a brief summary of the concepts, referring back to the book whenever necessary. In any case, remember that in Kabbalah inner change is the foundation of all growth. Everything that happens in the physical world is a reflection of our soul's progress on the path toward oneness with the Creator.

The story of one people—and of all people

In the Book of Genesis, the Creator gives Abram (later called Abraham) a very unusual command: "Go forth from your father's house to the land that I will show you." Abram isn't told why he should go forth, or exactly where he should go. The Creator does tell Abram, "I will make of you a great nation," but it's far from clear exactly what this means, how it will happen, or when it will happen. And at this time Abram is seventy-five years old and childless.

From a historical and literary perspective, this is unlike anything else that has come down to us from the ancient world. While there are many great stories of adventures and quests, the purpose is always clear: in the Babylonian epic of Gilgamesh, the hero sets forth to achieve immortality; in the *Iliad,* the Greeks go to war to recover a stolen queen; in the *Odyssey,* the Greek hero Odysseus overcomes both natural and supernatural obstacles to reach his home and family. Each of these tales has a clear goal, and each takes place within a well-defined time frame.

But the story of Abram and his descendants is very different. These people often don't know where they're going—and when they do, they don't know when they'll get there. Sometimes they're in one location for a long period of time, but often they're moving from one place to another. Sometimes they're slaves, while at other times they're rich and powerful. But the real constant in the biblical narrative is the inevitability of change. Again and again, the people of Israel experience the shattering of their world. The paradigm of the Light and the Vessel is both an expression of this experience and a revelation of its true meaning.

In this connection, it's clear that several of the true milestones in kabbalistic teaching have coincided with periods of persecution. We have already mentioned the expulsion from Spain at the end of the fifteenth century, which immediately preceded the work of Rabbi Isaac Luria, Rabbi Moses Cordovero, and Rabbi Chaim Vital. Similarly, Rabbi Yehuda Ashlag wrote *The Ten Luminous Emanations* and *Entrance to the Zohar* in the shadow of the Nazi genocide, perhaps the most brutal affliction ever inflicted on a people who have endured more than their share of suffering. Yet Rabbi Ashlag's ideas in no way contribute to a sense of passive victimization. On the contrary, it was Rabbi Ashlag who stressed the active nature of the Vessel in the Light and the Vessel paradigm. The Vessel itself initiated the restriction. The Vessel freely embraced the challenge of transforming its nature. We, as the Vessel's heirs, must accept and overcome the difficulties that we ourselves have chosen. This is a brave teaching, and not an easy one to embrace in the context of twentieth-century history. Rabbi Ashlag's teaching places responsibility for exile and dispersion in our hands—and in so doing, he shows that we also have the means to achieve transformation, redemption, and immortality.

None of the world's nations has been immune to tragedy. On the level of human history, the shattering of the Vessel has taken place again and again, and is still happening even today. Likewise, and perhaps even more importantly, the tools and teachings of Kabbalah are also available to all peoples regardless of their formal ethnic, national, or religious identity.

Kabbalah has often been identified as simply the esoteric tradition of Judaism, but this is very misleading. Kabbalah predates Judaism and all other religions and, as we've discussed, even predates creation itself. Kabbalah is no one's property. It was and is the gift of the Creator to all humanity.

The inner creation

The teachings of Kabbalah are not limited by the boundaries we accept in the everyday world, whether they divide one person from another or the material dimension from the spiritual. Individually and collectively, we start from the same place and move in the same direction, though along slightly different paths.

The paradigm of the Light and the Vessel describes every person's inner journey as well as the experience of humanity as a whole. At birth, the need to survive is paramount for every human being. A baby's body is a pure expression of the desire to receive for the self alone. Emotionally, too, children are bundles of need: for love, for support, for information, for protection, and for much more. But there comes a time when this dramatically shifts. Just as the primordial Vessel pushed back against the Light, in adolescence our orientation shifts from "need and more need" to "no need at all." A teenager is not really ready to follow through on this aspiration. Profound changes must take place before we reach true maturity. When we do, the desire to receive for the self alone that so dominated our early lives is now transformed into desire to receive for the purpose of sharing, very often with children of our own.

The Light and the Vessel is much more than a "creation myth" in an anthropological sense.

It's a way of understanding not only the creation of the physical universe, but also the process of self-creation in which each of us participates at every moment.

Even more remarkably, the Light and the Vessel teaches us that our individual experience ultimately hastens the transformation of the universe as a whole. As the teachings of Kabbalah emerge from centuries of obscurity and suppression, and as more and more people use these teachings to move from desire to receive for themselves toward desire to receive in order to share, a critical mass will come into being that will affect every aspect of reality. In this way, death itself will be brought to an end. The terrible, seemingly invincible power that so frightened me in that Safed motel will become powerless once and for all. And this will not be brought about by some chemical reaction in a test tube. It will be because of how you and I live our lives every moment of every day.

52

The death of death

For many people, the idea that our spiritual work can ultimately bring about "the death of death" is an extremely radical concept. Since it is also one of the foundations of all kabbalistic teaching, it deserves careful explanation. The kabbalists tell us that death can take place for some very different reasons. For example, when a very righteous person has completed his or her spiritual work on this plane of existence, he or she leaves the human form in order to enter a higher level of spirituality. From a kabbalistic standpoint, the death of such a person is hardly a time for sorrow and lamentation. It's not even an especially significant occasion: the essence of a truly righteous human being already resides in a higher realm, so departure from the physical body is almost a formality. But for less highly evolved people, the meaning of death can be quite different. Death takes place when spiritual transformation is no longer possible in this lifetime. When negative energy has accumulated to a degree that we've spiritually gone as far as we can go, the time comes for another revolution of what Rav Berg has called the Wheels of the Soul. In this sense, death is analogous to other cleansing experiences such as fasting. Death is a way of clearing the slate—of freeing the soul from the reactive encumbrances of the body so that the journey toward transformation can resume in a new incarnation.

The Rabbi and the Landowner

Once there was a famous rabbi who was renowned for his supernatural powers. A landowner from a nearby town sought him out one day and said, "Rabbi, I've heard of your ability to move back and forth between the past and the future, and to transport yourself across the oceans at the speed of lightning. But there's one talent that's been attributed to you that I would give anything to possess. It's your ability to talk with the animals. Do you think you could teach me that astonishing skill?"

The rabbi thought for a moment, then he said, "Well, perhaps I could teach you to do that. But are you sure it's something you really want to learn?"

"Oh yes!" said the landowner. "There's nothing I would rather do than talk with the creatures of the forests and the meadows. I beg of you! If it's in your power, please teach me the language of the animals, the birds, and even the fish!"

So the rabbi agreed, and the lessons actually took much less time than the landowner had imagined. In no time at all he was back at his home, ready to talk with the many wild creatures who lived nearby. In fact, he had not been home more than an hour before he struck up a conversation with a bird whose nest was not far from the landowner's doorway.

"I'm very pleased to make your acquaintance," said the bird, "but it so happens that there's a rather serious piece of information that I must share. I'm afraid that your house is going to be robbed tomorrow. The other day I heard some burglars planning it."

As a result of what the bird had told him, the landowner took elaborate preparations to safeguard his home. He hid several remote-controlled alarms in the bushes nearby, and he bought a shotgun with which to repel any intruders. Sure enough, the next day some burglars did set off the hidden alarms, but they quickly took flight when the landowner fired both barrels of his shotgun out the window of his home. Then, feeling much relieved, he lay down and took a long nap.

A few days later, however, as the landowner was taking a walk beside a small stream, a frog hopped into his path and spoke to him in very urgent tones: "Something very bad is going to happen unless you take action. I happen to know that your house is going to burn down because of sparks flying from the fireplace." And having said his piece, the frog hopped off.

Quickly returning home, the landowner inspected his fireplace and found that the newspapers he'd used for kindling were dangerously close to the grate. It would have been easy for sparks from burning logs to ignite the papers, from which a fire could quickly have spread to the curtains nearby. So he moved the papers. Certain of his safety, the landowner lit a cozy fire and took a nap in his easy chair. In fact, he slept all the way through to the next morning.

A week passed. Then one day the landowner stepped outside his front door to pick up the morning newspaper. Just then a squirrel came scampering up. "I don't think you'll have time today to read the news," said the squirrel. "Your time has come to leave this world."

The landowner was shocked! How could this be possible? Yet everything the animals told him had come true. So the panic-stricken landowner raced off to the rabbi's house to find out what this dire prediction could possibly mean. Arriving a few hours later, he informed the rabbi of what the squirrel had said—only to see the rabbi sadly shake his head.

"There's nothing I can do," he said. "As you know, I was not eager to teach you to speak with birds, frogs, and squirrels, and now you see why. It's true that they helped you avert some serious setbacks in your material well-being, but it's also true that those setbacks were put into your life in order to help you grow as a spiritual being. Now the spiritual work that was left unaccomplished in this lifetime will have to be taken up in another."

If the opportunity to return to the world in a new incarnation seems to diminish the significance of death, that is certainly not the intention of this fundamental kabbalistic teaching. On the contrary, the continued presence of death *at all* in the world proves that much spiritual progress urgently remains to be achieved. Just as death came into being at the sin of Adam, it can likewise be eliminated through our own spiritual work—and this is a collective enterprise of all humanity. Although over the course of history a small number of righteous people have merited freedom from death, few of us will attain the spiritual level of Moses or Elijah. Instead, we can work as individuals to bring about the transformation of the world as a whole. As each of us evolves to higher levels of spirituality, the Light we reveal will facilitate others' evolution as well, and ultimately the final redemption of mankind will be achieved.

If immortality is not available to us now, Kabbalah assures us—guarantees us—that the death of death is indeed on its way. How soon it arrives is entirely up to us.

It's not easy. Transformation doesn't happen automatically. It begins with *awareness* and with *desire*—two fundamental resources of spiritual energy: We are aware that we come from God, and at the very core of our being we *desire* to regain this unity. And God desires it for us as well.

The Hebrew word *d'vekut* expresses this desire. It refers to such a close bonding with the Creator that no separation remains. In our everyday lives, we are like stones that have been carried away from an enormous mountain. We assume individual identities for a time, but when we return to our point of origin we are no longer separate objects. We are again part of the mountain. This is exactly what takes place when a human soul achieves *d'vekut*. Separation from the Creator is recognized as an illusion, and Oneness is revealed as the supreme truth.

The Upper Worlds

Kabbalah teaches that the physical and spiritual dimensions are intimately interwoven. As a kabbalistic precept puts it, "As above, so below." Just as we are influenced by the spiritual realm, our actions in everyday life directly affect what kabbalists call the Upper Worlds. This phrase, however, requires some explanation. In Kabbalah, time and distance are understood in terms of proximity to the Creator. The great kabbalists were close to the Upper Worlds not in the sense that they could fly through the air (though there are tales that some of them could!), but because their souls were developed to supremely high spiritual levels. The Upper Worlds exist within ourselves, in the sense that each of us is a expression of all creation.

This is a genuinely holographic concept of the universe and our place in it—and it was fully developed in Kabbalah thousands of years before anyone had heard of holograms.

Even if a hologram is shattered, every fragment of it contains the entire image, just as each of us embodies the totality of the shattered primordial Vessel. What's more, each fragment of a hologram shows the image at a slightly different angle, just as each of us must follow our own unique path to transformation.

You have to earn it

Thorough the centuries, humanity's greatest minds have grappled with the nature of God and the questions raised by our seemingly fragile existence. For what purpose, it's often been asked, did the Creator let everything get so complicated? Why does spiritual transformation have to be so difficult? If there is no limit to God's power, why doesn't God just instantly reinvent us as a species of six billion Rabbi Lurias, each a fully enlightened human soul?

Answering this question takes us to a central kabbalistic insight:

We cannot achieve fulfillment without doing the spiritual work of earning fulfillment.

Our essence is of the Creator, whose nature is to give and to share, and for whom the whole concept of "free gifts" is inadmissible. There is a Hebrew phrase in the Talmud that is pertinent to this idea—*nahama dichisufa,* which can be translated as "bread of shame." It refers to wealth or sustenance that, because it is unearned, brings us pain and regret rather than joy and fulfillment. Rabbi Ashlag called attention to this phrase as a way of describing the dangers of unmerited abundance. On a spiritual level, and psychologically as well, it's against our interests and against our nature to accept "something for nothing."

Suppose the wealthiest man in the world decided to start an art collection. Nothing prevents him from calling an auction house and simply ordering up all the greatest paintings in the world. "Just send them over and mail me a bill," he could say, amazed at how easy it is to become an art collector. But of course he would have completely missed the real experience of art collecting. The objects he acquired would have no real value, since they were acquired without effort, thought, or feeling. The purpose of collecting art, therefore, is clearly not just a matter of getting paintings and sculptures into your house. The real purpose is the journey that had to be undertaken in order to reach the goal. The Creator needs us to make our own way toward Him—not because He "can't" have it otherwise, but because the process is what's really essential.

Rav Berg sometimes uses another metaphor to make the same point. According to football lore, the great coach Vince Lombardi of the Green Bay Packers once said, "Winning isn't everything. It's the only thing." But is this really true, even within the limited sphere of competitive athletics? Suppose Vince Lombardi had asked a great kabbalist for a special blessing that would allow the Packers to win every single game without fail. Season after season, year after year, Green Bay would just keep on winning. Would Vince Lombardi really be happy? Would his players feel motivated to give their best effort? Would the fans in the stadium continue to turn out and applaud the team? Of course not—because the risk of defeat is what gives value to the experience of victory. If winning were *really* the only thing, it would quickly become meaningless.

Fortunately for us, transformation is not a "sure thing." It's an ongoing challenge and opportunity. To help us meet this challenge, the Creator has given us the tools of Kabbalah—which is not to say that it's easy. As human beings, we're the ones who must struggle with the pains of mortal existence. We're the ones who must face disease and death. Who among us, at difficult moments, might not wish that the gates of heaven would just swing open and an angel would shout, "Come on in!"

But would it really be better? Imagine that a wealthy man passes on and leaves an enormous fortune to his son. Does this guarantee the son's happiness? Does this ensure that the son will feel fulfilled and satisfied with his life? Should we expect that the son will instantly gain a great soul just as he has instantly gained great riches? Obviously not, because emotional and spiritual growth are the products of time and struggle, not of a sudden increase in the bank balance. And there's a strong argument that people who work hard throughout their lives and provide for their families are more likely to be spiritually advanced than those to whom everything has come easily.

We must come to understand that life's challenges are opportunities for growth, not mere afflictions that God ought to get rid of for us. Our purpose in this world is to achieve oneness with the Creator through spiritual work using the tools of Kabbalah that have been provided for us. There is no quick fix, nor should we long for one. Spiritual fulfillment cannot be a gift. We must earn it; we must work for it.

PART TWO

Getting Ready for the Light

CHAPTER 4

The Work
of Living

W"ork" refers to more than such purely spiritual disciplines as meditation or even prayer. Kabbalah's understanding of this derives from the opening chapters of the Bible. Following the sin of Adam, "The Creator sent Adam out from the Garden of Eden to work the land from which he was taken." From this verse the kabbalistic sages inferred that Adam's work had earlier been on the spiritual plane only, but that now he undertook physical work as well. For us, the lesson is that no spiritual growth can be achieved without positive action in the physical world.

Many people arrive at a point in their lives in which they sincerely want to reach a higher level of spiritual awareness. They're eager to think, study, and meditate—and they're correct in realizing that inner change is the essential foundation for connecting to the Light. But it's deceptively easy to think that this provides license to disengage from the hard work of living in the everyday world, or even from the work of living inside a human body, with all its needs and demands. Our interactions with the physical world, and with our physical selves, are our real opportunities for encountering and eventually transforming the desire to receive for ourselves alone. Rather than avoiding this encounter, we should take full advantage of it.

The Inner Game of Tennis, a bestselling book some years ago, made the point that success or failure in sports is strongly influenced by athletes' expectations, emotions, and levels of stress. This book was one of the first to emphasize the benefits of techniques such as breath control and meditation. But suppose someone became so entranced by the inner game of tennis that he never got around to the outer game—from which, after all, there is also a great deal to be learned. This is what happens to a significant number of people who become interested in spiritual development. It may even be exactly what they want to happen: perhaps unconsciously, they see spirituality as an *alternative* to the complexities of the physical world.

According to kabbalistic teaching, however, spiritual growth and the work of everyday life are interdependent and inseparable. Regarding this, kabbalistic texts sometimes describe the human souls as being encased within a multilayered, opaque shell. Within the shell, the soul may be very highly developed. Perhaps it's even a great soul, capable of drawing a great Light. But until the physical work of breaking the shell takes place, transformation can't take place. The Light can't be received.

The one-directional pathway

We've spoken a great deal about transformation, and it may be useful to reiterate exactly what this means. Kabbalah teaches that we are in this world to transform *desire to receive for the self alone* into *desire to receive for the purpose of sharing,* and thereby to achieve oneness with the Creator. Anything negative that happens in this world, whether to an individual or to humanity as a whole, is a manifestation of self-centered desire. The more we are connected to the desire to receive for ourselves, the greater our disconnection from the Light. Self-serving desire is the single barrier that separates us from the Creator. It is the great challenge that we face in our journey of transformation. It is the mountain we must climb and the ocean we must cross.

It may surprise you to learn that a positive outcome to this journey is guaranteed.

In both spirituality and biology, evolution only takes place in one direction. Neither our bodies, nor our brains, nor our souls can reverse course—but this point is perhaps easier to grasp in terms of the species than of the spirit. The evolutionary biologist Stephen Jay Gould, for example, wrote his doctoral dissertation on the fact that there are today only six basic designs of seashells. These six are the survivors of hundreds of other designs that fell by the wayside during the process of natural selection. That process, of course, is still continuing. It's not inconceivable that someday there will be five kinds of shells, or even only one. But there will never be seven or seven hundred, just as there will never be any more Cro-Magnon or Neanderthal men.

According to Kabbalistic teachings, our souls are evolving along a similarly one-directional pathway. At the same time, however, there is a fundamental difference between Kabbalah's view of our spiritual evolution and the Darwinian process of natural selection. According to Darwin, progress takes place in evolution largely by accident. In an often-cited example, the giraffe did not evolve a long neck in order to eat leaves from the top of a tree. Rather, a particularly long-necked giraffe happened to be born and had an advantage over its shorter-necked competitors. When it reproduced, its offspring had a similar advantage, did well in the struggle for survival, and eventually all giraffes had long necks. This did not take place in accordance with any underlying intention or grand plan of Nature. It just happened.

But our spiritual evolution has a purpose and a goal, which is the final and infinite union of God and man ordained by God at the time of creation, and forestalled by the sin of Adam.

Proactive versus reactive

Every soul will reach the objective, though no two souls will do so in exactly the same way, because there are as many approaches to transformation as there are variations in faces or voices or fingerprints. Within this infinite variety of experiences, however, there are two basic paths, which Kabbalah calls *proactive* and *reactive.* As human beings, we must choose between these two means to the same end. We can transform *proactively,* by nurturing the desire to share that is our bond with the Creator. Or we can stand apart from the Creator by building our lives around the desire to receive for the self alone. We can proactively use the tools of Kabbalah that God has given us, or we can achieve transformation *in reaction* to hardship, pain, confusion, and suffering. The ability to make this choice is the only genuine free will that anyone has. Once we've exercised our power of choice, we have the ability to make changes in our lives that express the choice we've made. Making these changes is not always easy. By surmounting the difficulties, we earn and deserve the outcome that we desire. If our choices were made for us or if the difficulties were magically removed, we would never earn anything. We would be puppets rather than people.

So what shall we choose—between living reactively or proactively, between selfish desire and desire to share? The correct option seems so obvious—but the desire to receive for the self alone is like a highly addictive drug. We're hooked on the euphoria it can provide. The drug has become so much a part of our lives that we're not even aware we're using it anymore!

Like other drugs, self-serving desire has many street names. Money, Fame, and Power are some of the most familiar. Even Humiliation and Defeat can have a powerful allure, if only unconsciously. But the same energy underlies all of them, and there's no denying that it can provide much pleasure and excitement. In fact, for many people this is the only version of happiness they've ever known. Giving it up is inconceivable.

But like any addictive substance, the pleasurable effects of the desire to receive for the self alone are transitory and increasingly short-lived. The more we use it and the more we come to depend upon it, the less satisfaction we feel. Eventually we find ourselves on an increasingly dark metaphysical street at all hours of the night, looking for more Fame, more Power, more Money, more Recognition, more Love, more Status. Or perhaps more Pain and Suffering. But no matter how much we get, the euphoria wears off and we're back where we started from. These can be very difficult habits to break. After all, receiving for ourselves is our primary tendency—and the sharing doesn't always provide the same rush of immediate gratification.

Going against our nature

In order to transform our desire to receive for ourselves alone into desire to receive for the purpose of sharing, we must first recognize how much of our nature is rooted in the need for sensation and immediate gratification. Then we must make a conscious, determined effort to transcend those needs in favor of much greater ones.

As a long-concealed and supremely powerful body of wisdom, it's not surprising that Kabbalah counsels us to pay special attention to all that is subtle and hidden, and to guard ourselves against overwhelming enthusiasm for all that is obvious and fully disclosed. The truth never shouts. It speaks to us in whispers. We must make a determined effort to hear the truth over the noise and negativity that pervade our world. Our task is to attune ourselves to the frequency of true wisdom and to train ourselves to hear it through the static that distracts so much of the world.

As always in Kabbalah, this training does not happen by itself—but once it's accomplished, there are immense rewards. The world is so constructed that almost every opportunity for proactivity and sharing first presents itself as quite the opposite. If you find a wallet with a hundred dollars inside, what's your first impulse? When another driver cuts you off on the road, what do you immediately want to do? When someone speaks harshly to you, is your first reflex to respond peacefully and patiently? These, of course, are rather obvious situations, and most of us learn to deal with them in a proactive manner. But true sharing is fundamentally more challenging. Initially, at least, true sharing is painful in the way any growth is painful.

Kabbalah's definition of sharing is fundamentally different from our everyday understanding of the word. For example, sacrificing our own comfort for family and friends can be a positive act, but it's not necessarily a transforming act because it does not often go against our nature. It's even tempting to say that "no pain, no gain" is a kabbalistic principle. But true sharing does not really involve pain, any more than self-centered action brings real happiness. It's simply a matter of recognizing the resistance to transformation that's inherent in our nature as human beings, and then confronting that resistance with full consciousness and determination.

In order for parents to provide food and shelter for their children, hard work and sacrifice are often required. But this sort of sharing is not really counter to the parents' inclinations. On the contrary, nurturing children is encoded in our nature as human beings. It satisfies a need in parents just as it does for their offspring. Parenting, therefore, is certainly a noble and even a sacred endeavor, but it is not really a transforming one. It requires no basic change in our nature.

Sharing is natural when it feels good, or even because it

feels good. For this reason, Kabbalah tells us to share when it's uncomfortable. When you're countering the inertia of your everyday nature, when you're going against the reflex of your own immediate gratification, you are moving toward real spiritual growth and transformation. This is not to suggest you should stop sharing when it feels good. But it does mean that sharing to transform your nature is by definition *uncomfortable.*

We are like runners training for a marathon. Wind sprints and weight lifting can cause discomfort, but they increase our ability to successfully complete a long and challenging race. Each time we challenge ourselves to share, we take a step toward oneness with the Creator and the true fulfillment that it brings. Each act of true sharing breaks down the barriers of our desire to receive for the self alone and liberates the infinitely deeper and richer experience of sharing that is hidden within us.

Positive and negative, light and dark

Kabbalah views each of us as balanced between two powerful forces. A positive force draws us toward transformation of our nature and ultimate fulfillment, while a corresponding negative energy impels us toward self-serving action, instant gratification, and transitory pleasure.

Both these forces are acting on us in equal measure all the time. The significance of the positive force is self-evident, but the negative force is also indispensable to our spiritual development.

Because of the negative force, we have an opportunity to choose the direction of our lives at every moment. Remember: choice makes it possible for us to earn the Creator's benefi-cence. Without choice, lasting fulfillment is impossible.

Just as we confront these two forces as individuals, human-ity also stands balanced between them. We are literally "all in this together." Kabbalah teaches that when even one human being chooses the positive direction, the world as a whole also moves toward the Light. On a very practical level, our positive deeds allow others to act in ways that would not have been pos-sible had we not acted. And likewise, when we move toward the negative side of selfishness and self-interest, the world tilts toward negativity.

In this way, each of us is intimately involved with the for-tunes of all of us. Our positive and negative actions, no matter how small, influence the spiritual state of the world.

This brings up a major kabbalistic principle:

The external awakens the internal.

Resisting our self-serving nature in everyday life is an exter-nal act that awakens our own inner potential, and that of every-one else as well. The goal of transformation, for ourselves and for the world, is to *be* different. But we can each make a good start by *behaving* differently on our own.

We're all in the same boat

Consider this: two friends went fishing in a small rowboat. When they reached the middle of the lake, one man was surprised to see the other drilling a hole in the bottom of the boat. "What are you doing making a hole like that?" the first man screamed. But the second man just looked at him calmly and replied: "Don't worry, it's only under my seat."

Clearly, the second man had never studied Kabbalah! Still, in contemporary terms he might very well consider himself a spiritual person who's just doing his own thing. The shared nature of our spiritual destiny is a significant point of divergence between Kabbalah and other teachings. Transformation, as we've seen, is really about learning to share with others. It's the furthest thing possible from the "me-centered" focus that's often associated with New Age teachings.

Our goal, our purpose, and our only reason for being in the world is to transform our desire to receive for ourselves alone into a desire to share—and by doing so, to become one with the Creator. We do this because ultimately it is in our own best interests. But beyond transforming ourselves, Kabbalah teaches that we are responsible for the world's spiritual transformation as well. As long as even one of us falls short of the goal, all of us fall short. We're all in the same boat. If one person is sinking, we are all sinking.

This concept is explicitly derived from the paradigm of the Light and the Vessel. When the primordial Vessel shattered into an infinite number of pieces, the fragments became the matter and energy that comprise the physical world. Everything that we see, hear, taste, smell, or even think about is part of the original Vessel. We ourselves are the Vessel, and therefore everything that exists in the physical realm is part of us.

Take action in the real world

From this realization comes a very specific insight into how we can best live our lives:

At least half of what we do in the world ought to be directed toward assisting others. This supremely important work can take many forms, but Kabbalah explicitly teaches that practical action is at least as worthwhile as piety or righteous observance. Feeding a hungry person is just as likely to bring transformation as prayer or meditation. Simply put, Kabbalah requires us to *take real action in the real world.*

But doing this from a kabbalistic perspective involves more than just running out to perform "good deeds." True sharing requires a basic shift in the way we see our lives and our relationships to the people around us. Quite naturally, most of us have learned to see our lives as ongoing stories, with ourselves as the main character. We try to move the plot forward toward our goals, which for many people are defined in material terms: a beautiful home, a substantial income, recognition for personal and professional achievements. These are certainly worthwhile aspirations, but Kabbalah cautions us against making them the primary focus of our being, especially at the expense of others. And Kabbalah also offers ways of understanding our lives that are positive alternatives to the heroic sagas most of us strive to construct.

Put together the jigsaw puzzle

From a kabbalistic viewpoint, there are many advantages to thinking of life as a kind of puzzle—a jigsaw or a crossword—

rather than as a linear narrative. We've learned to see stories as finished when the main character (that's you!) reaches a resolution. But suppose we were to ask what happened to all the other characters: the taxi driver in Chapter 1, the airplane pilot in Chapter 4, the little girl who picked a flower on the last page of the book? Kabbalah tells us that the "story" isn't really complete until *everyone* is accounted for—that is, until *everyone* has achieved spiritual transformation. The metaphor of life as a story makes this difficult to grasp. Stories must of necessity distinguish between the importance of their characters. We can—in fact, we must—accept the idea that a story is finished when the major players have reached their objectives. A jigsaw puzzle, on the other hand, is obviously not complete until every piece is in its place. Moreover, attention to one part of the puzzle does not mean lack of attention to the other parts: the *whole thing* must be attended to, or none of it is a success.

An incident in the Bible illuminates this point. In Chapter 37 of the Book of Genesis, Jacob instructs his seventeen-year-old son Joseph to travel to the valley of Hebron to "see how your brothers are, and how the flocks are faring." But when Joseph arrives at the destination, his brothers are nowhere to be seen. Just then a man comes walking by. The Bible does not even give him a name, yet in a sense the whole biblical narrative depends on him. He's the small piece of the puzzle without which its completion would be impossible. "What are you looking for?" asks this nameless man, and when Joseph replies that he's looking for his brothers, the nameless man says, "They have gone from here, for I heard them say, 'Let us go to Dothan.'" Then the nameless man disappears back into the ranks of the great unsung characters of literature. He also ascends back into the Upper Worlds, for Kabbalah teaches that he was in fact the angel Gabriel.

As an individual human being, you have a dual nature: you are putting the puzzle together, but you are also one of the pieces. You must further the completion of the puzzle both by finding your own place and by finding places for the other fragments. It doesn't matter how long it takes, it doesn't matter how many mistakes or frustrations you encounter before you finish your work—in fact, the setbacks will only make the completion even more satisfying. But you must learn to see the unity of your own interests with the interests of everyone around you. You are all part of the same Vessel that was shattered and that must again be made whole.

The source of pain and suffering

We've spoken about the difficulty of transforming our desire to receive into desire to receive in order to share. But "difficulty" is not a strong enough word to describe what many people face in their lives, and it's often not easy to see how their problems can be ascribed to anything like selfishness on their part. There is real pain in the world. And outside the developed countries of the West, there is pain on a scale that many of us can hardly imagine.

How does Kabbalah integrate this fact with the idea of a loving and beneficent God? This is an extremely good question, and even an urgent one. It deserves a clear and direct response.

Before we discuss the meaning of pain and suffering in the

world, we should identify their source. If the Creator is wholly good and all things derive from Him, how does Kabbalah explain the presence of all that seems to be evil in the world? If the Creator is purely positive, where did the negative presence come from?

Kabbalah teaches that two forces are at work in the world. The positive force is the Light of the Creator, but a negative side also exists, to allow us to truly face the test of choosing between good and evil and to have free will in making that choice. The negative side—often called "the evil inclination" in kabbalistic teachings—is the force that tries to push us to do actions that are based on the desire to receive for the self alone. The positive side is the force that tries to assist us to transform and become beings of sharing. Both these forces are within every single one of us in equal measure. At every moment we have free will in choosing which inclination we will follow.

In the study of the world's spiritual systems, a key distinction is made between those that present evil as independent and opposite from good and those that believe that evil is a corrupt or otherwise degraded version of the Creator's benevolence. Wars and persecutions have taken place over this issue—which must have been gratifying to the power of evil no matter where it came from!

What is evil?

Kabbalah's understanding of evil is beautifully illustrated by a parable from the Zohar. A king wanted to test the character of his son, to see whether he was worthy to inherit the kingdom.

In order to do this, the king sought out the most disreputable harlot in the land, and he instructed her to try to seduce his son. But should he also instruct her to reveal the fact that she's working for the king? Of course not, because in that case there would be no test. The harlot would immediately lose her power over the prince. Far from seeing her as an evil temptress, he would understand that she was another loyal servant of the ruler.

Each of us is like the prince in that parable. Each of us is faced with the most severe temptations, but what is the real source of the temptation? What really makes it seem so dangerous and compelling? Kabbalah teaches that evil resides in our perception of evil. If we understood its true origin and purpose, it would be revealed as another manifestation of the Creator's wisdom.

Until I read this parable, I had always wondered about the teaching that a truly righteous individual sees no evil in any other human beings regardless of how they might appear to the rest of the world. Considering some of the things that people have done over the course of human history, how could anyone *not* recognize them as evil? That capacity seemed less like an attribute of righteousness than a form of blindness. But as the parable of the harlot makes clear, it's not that a righteous person does not see evil at all, but that he or she sees it differently than the rest of the world. A righteous person sees evil not as an independent phenomenon, but as a powerful testing instrument of the Creator.

Kabbalah tells us that the great sage Rabbi Akiva was just such a righteous person. Rabbi Akiva, who lived in the second century C.E., was a shepherd until the age of forty, whereupon he began to follow a spiritual path. In the year 132, following a Jewish rebellion against the Romans, who ruled Palestine, it was decreed that Rabbi Akiva should be put to death in a public execution. On the day when the sentence was to be carried out, Rabbi Akiva confronted this terrible evil like the great kabbalist he was. On the way to the execution, the rabbi's students were in disbelief that such a thing could be happening to this great and good man. Yet Rabbi Akiva was unconcerned about who was responsible for this great injustice. In fact, he was perfectly serene. Though he admitted he did not know what he could have done to bring this about, he refused to blame anyone else. This may seem astonishing to a modern reader, living in an age when the role of victim has become so very tempting, but it is completely consistent with kabbalistic principles. Moreover, when the actual execution was about to take place and another student was lamenting the tragedy, Rabbi Akiva sternly told him to be silent—and then he added, "This is the greatest moment of my life."

What is the teaching here? How can a completely innocent man proclaim his own murder as the greatest moment of his life? In what sense could such an atrocity possibly be called *great*? What Rabbi Akiva meant, I believe, was that he had been given an opportunity to confront evil in its purest manifestation, and he had been *up to the task*. He refused to acknowledge evil as a malignant power in its own right. He freely chose instead to see even the worst acts of his enemies as a form of service to the Creator. They had provided him with an opportunity to comport himself with courage and certainty, and thereby to reveal more Light in the world. By no means was

Rabbi Akiva blind or oblivious to evil. On the contrary, he had the strength to see it for what it truly was and still is.

There are spiritual laws

Here we should recall a key point made earlier:

We are not the Creator's puppets. We are partners with the Creator in the great ongoing process of Creation—and we ourselves are the source of all pain and tragedy. Our negative actions, our negative desires, our negative thoughts, bring sorrow into our own lives and into the world.

For many people, humanity's own ultimate responsibility for suffering is perhaps the most difficult of all Kabbalah's precepts. We just naturally resist this idea. We deny our responsibility with all our might. We're infinitely more comfortable blaming some external force or being—or we might even imagine a world where there's no cause for anything at all. We might prefer no cause at all to taking responsibility for ourselves. Perhaps the universe is just a random sequence of events.

In order to understand kabbalistic teaching in this critical area, consider the following imaginary sequence of events. During a visit to New York, a young woman visits the Empire State Building. Just for a lark, she decides to jump off. As she falls, the sensation is genuinely thrilling. But when she hits the pavement, she breaks both her legs. The thrill is over and the pain has started.

Who bears responsibility for this woman's troubles? Most of us would say without hesitation that the woman herself is at fault. She wasn't pushed, and no one told her to jump, but she jumped anyway. Case closed.

Would anyone blame the law of gravity in this situation? That would seem very unreasonable. Even though we can't see it, even though there are no signs posted on bridges or at the top of tall buildings cautioning us about the physics of falling objects, we know very well that gravity is in effect. If we decide to jump off a building or bridge, we encounter the consequences very soon after taking the leap.

Disregarding the law of gravity is plainly foolish and dangerous.

And this is true of spiritual laws as well. Spiritual laws are every bit as inexorable as the principles of physics or chemistry—yet it's somehow more difficult for us to accept the idea that spiritual laws have the same cause-and-effect pattern.

Let's be very clear about this. If you choose to disregard spiritual law—if you act in a negative manner and if your life is governed by desire to receive for yourself alone—you are disconnecting from the Light of the Creator. Unless your destructive behavior is countered and corrected by your own positive action, Kabbalah teaches that pain of some sort will result. That's the law, and there's no getting around it.

The element of choice

There is, however, one major difference between the laws of cause and effect in spirituality and in the natural sciences. In the everyday world, it usually takes only one jump off a bridge to realize the foolishness of the endeavor. The negative result is apparent in just a few seconds. Yet we can take a number of spiritually reckless leaps without ever hitting the pavement. We can experience the thrill of the jump and not feel the pain, at least not for a while.

The reason for this time lag between cause and effect in the realm of spirituality is simple and very revealing. It pertains to the free will that defines us as human beings and as partners with God in the ongoing process of creation.

If we lived in a world where the effects of negative action were immediately manifested as pain and suffering, the element of choice would disappear from our lives.

To understand this, imagine that every negative action was immediately punished by a powerful electric shock. It would not take long for negativity to disappear from human behavior—but it would be because of *suppression*, not *choice*. Right action would flow from fear of punishment, not from positive and proactive decision. The free will that the Creator ordained for us would disappear.

With respect to the spiritual laws, the correlation between cause and effect is concealed in order to preserve our power of choice.

So we are not immediately shocked by electricity every time we move in the wrong spiritual direction. We are also not instantly rewarded whenever we choose the right action. Instead, it's up to us to develop awareness of our behavior and its relationship to spiritual law. It's up to us to make decisions and choices—and to realize that consequences, both good and bad, will eventually develop from our actions. When painful consequences do materialize, we may be mystified by the causes. When we are most confused, we may even blame the Creator—but this is as ludicrous as blaming the law of gravity for the pain of hitting the pavement when you jump off a roof.

Pain is an opportunity for us to correct our behavior.

Wheels of the Soul

When the Baal Shem Tov was living in the town of Medzhibozh, in Poland, it was said that this righteous man had the power to cure all sorts of problems. One day he was visited by a merchant from a nearby town. The merchant told the Baal Shem Tov his troubles, expecting to get a blessing right there on the spot that would alleviate his distress. Instead, the Baal Shem Tov told the merchant to travel to the little town of Trusti and ask for a man named Eliezer ben Zerah.

The merchant was disconcerted by this advice. "Trusti? Trusti is a journey of three days and nights along a very bad road. Can't you take care of my troubles right here?" But the Baal Shem Tov insisted, "Go to Trusti and ask for Eliezer ben Zerah. He will help you." Reluctantly, the merchant did as he was told.

The trip to Trusti was long indeed. Along the way, the merchant had plenty of time to think about all the possible reasons that the Baal Shem Tov had sent him on such an uncomfortable journey. "This Eliezer ben Zerah," he thought, "he must be a very great man indeed if the Baal Shem Tov sends me to him. And if he is a great man, he *might* be a rich man as well. Yes, of course, that is why I am going to see him! He is a rich man who is going to give me money to solve my financial problems! And if he is rich, well, then, he must have sons. One of these sons is probably a perfect match for my daughter, who thinks no man is good enough. Yes, I'm certain of it! This is the reason I am going to Trusti. The Baal Shem Tov is a genius."

So it was that the merchant arrived in the tiny town of Trusti with great expectations of what the wealthy Eliezer ben Zerah was about to do for him. The merchant hopped out of the carriage and asked the livery man, "Eliezer ben Zerah. Where does he live?" But the livery man didn't know the name. "How could you not know Eliezer ben Zerah? A great man, a rich man, with sons, many sons!" But the livery man just shrugged, "I don't know him. Why don't you ask the butcher? He knows everybody." And he directed the merchant to the butcher's house.

But the butcher didn't know Eliezer ben Zerah either. And worse, neither did the postman, and even worse, neither did the local rabbi. "How can this be?" the merchant whined. "The great Baal Shem Tov himself sent me here to ask for Eliezer ben Zerah. He's supposed to help me." The rabbi was sympathetic. "Look," he said, "one of the women in my congregation is over a hundred years old, but she's still very, very sharp in the head. She's lived here her whole life and she knows the whole history of Trusti and everyone that ever lived in the town. If anyone knows this Eliezer ben Zerah, she will."

So the rabbi escorted the merchant to the old woman and they asked her about Eliezer ben Zerah. A glimmer of recognition passed over her face. "Eliezer ben Zerah?" she said. "Yes, yes," the merchant said, excited by the prospect of finally finding someone who knew the name. The old woman stood up, approached the merchant, looked him in the eye, and said, "He was the worst." She spit on the ground. "He was rotten! He beat his wife. He beat his children. He ran around. He abused his animals. He drank. He punched the rabbi in the nose. Everybody hated him. He never did a good thing in his entire life. I don't even want to talk about him. When he died, half the town celebrated."

"He died?" the shocked merchant said, "When?"

"Fifty-seven years ago," the old woman replied. "That's why no one else remembers. They are too young."

The merchant was very upset. Here he was expecting all his troubles to be solved, he had traveled all this way, and now he found that the person who was supposed to help him was not only a rotten drunkard, but worse, had been dead for fifty-seven years.

All the way back to Medzhibozh he stewed and steamed about it, so that by the time he returned to the Baal Shem Tov, the merchant was very, very angry. "What kind of trick is this?" the merchant shouted. "Don't you know I'm a very busy man? I traveled all the way to Trusti for nothing. You wasted my time! I thought this Eliezer ben Zerah was supposed to help me? I didn't get any money. He didn't have any sons for my daughter. I didn't even get a blessing. The man is dead."

The Baal Shem Tov waited for the merchant to calm down and then said, "I never said anything about money, or sons. But the blessing, that you did get."

"What blessing? How could I get a blessing from a dead man?"

"How old are you?" the Baal Shem Tov suddenly asked.

"How old am I? I'm fifty-six years old. What does my age have to do with anything?"

And then the Baal Shem Tov said, "I want you to know that in your previous life, Eliezer ben Zerah was you. Knowing how terrible you were in your last incarnation, you should thank the Creator every day for giving you so much in this life. All your troubles now are a result of your behavior then. Believe me, as bad as you were, it could be a lot worse. The blessing is the knowledge that you're getting another chance despite what you did last time."

Use your time well

When we come into this world, we are given the *exact* amount of time that's necessary to complete our spiritual work. Each of us has specific tasks to perform, and your tasks may be different from mine, but Kabbalah tells us that our transformation can be completed in one lifetime. We have enough time, but we also don't have any time to waste. As we come to understand how big our task really is, we will also understand that we can never let up—we can never become complacent in our spiritual work. If an athlete knows he needs to run only a mile each day, he will undoubtedly take his time—he may even go out to a movie before doing his short run. But if he knows that his training requires a daily twenty-mile run, running will become the organizing principle of his day and the central experience of his life. This is true also of our spiritual work. We have no time to spare, and we must build our entire lives toward achieving transformation.

Unfortunately, most of us don't use our time very well. Everyday life distracts us from our larger purpose. As the years pass, we may achieve part of our transformation, or perhaps none at all. But the fact is, most of us depart this life without completing the task we came here to do. We may even have moved in the opposite direction, away from the Light of the Creator.

Kabbalah teaches that we will return to this world in many incarnations until we achieve complete transformation.

Work left uncompleted in this life is undertaken again in a future life until the task of transformation is done. Reincarnation is a fundamental tenet of Kabbalah. The world and our place in it cannot be understood without this key principle.

As always, what is true for a single human soul is also true for all humanity. As long as you or I fall short of transformation, we will continue to participate in the cycle of birth, death, and rebirth—as will mankind as a whole, until the critical mass of truly enlightened people comes into being to eradicate pain and death forever.

The possibility of reincarnation is not a license to ignore our spiritual responsibilities in this life. On the contrary, reincarnation should be an incentive to complete our spiritual tasks as quickly as possible, to attend to the work of transformation, and to live more sharing, compassionate lives. Only in this way can we get off the wheel of arrival and departure in the world, and get rid of the pain that inevitably comes with it.

In the next chapter we'll begin applying the spiritual tools of Kabbalah toward building a relationship with the Creator, and in subsequent sections, we'll apply the tools to life in the every-day world. Right now, however, be sure you understand the paradigm of the Light and the Vessel and the other ideas we've covered so far. It might be useful to look again through these earlier chapters before going further in the book. Again, explaining the ideas to a friend or family member in your own words can also help clarify your own understanding. Or, as I suggested before, you might try writing a brief summary of the concepts, referring back to the book whenever necessary. In any case, remember that in Kabbalah, *spirit* is always the foundation. Everything that happens in the physical world is a reflection of our soul's progress (or lack of progress) on the path toward oneness with God.

With that in mind, we can look more closely at what it means to live in full awareness of the Creator's presence and the Creator's love.

CHAPTER 5

Building a Relationship with the Creator

Transforming our desire to receive for ourselves into a desire to share is the hardest task we will ever attempt. But remember: Every positive action we perform, every empathic thought that passes through our minds, every emotion of love and caring in our hearts, brings forth the Light and moves us closer to oneness with the Creator.

Even seemingly insignificant acts of empathy and sharing are enormously meaningful. This brings up an interesting kabbalistic principle: what seems small in the physical realm often looms large in the spiritual dimension; what is hidden in the physical world may be hugely prominent in the world above. Just as infinitely small atomic particles contain vast resources of energy, well-concealed positive thoughts, deeds, and feelings are of supreme spiritual value. Conversely, even well-camou-flaged expressions of selfishness or insensitivity move us away from the Light toward chaos, pain, and death.

As you now undertake your journey of transformation with full awareness of both the obstacles and the opportunities, there is a single truth that you absolutely must take to heart.

You must realize and accept how desperately you need the Creator's help.

Ego tells us that we are alone in the world—that we can and must do everything ourselves. Ego seeks to distance us from the Light of the Creator, and perhaps to deny the existence of the Light altogether. For this reason, simply acknowledging our need for the Creator's help can be a major step in the right direction. This is the first whisper that we are not alone, the first step in building a relationship with the Creator, and the first crack in the shell of ego that imprisons the Light within us. When we recognize our need for God's assistance, we create an ego-free space within ourselves. Kabbalah describes this as *creating a Vessel into which the Light can flow.* And the greater our realization of the need for help, the more help we are able to receive.

A Great Gift, Well Disguised

Many years ago, a small businessman named Nathan was in terrible financial straits. He was deeply in debt, but because of his large family and the expenses that came with it he was continuously having to borrow more money. But finally the sources of borrowed money dried up. No one would lend him anything more, and he still had to pay interest on what he had borrowed previously. In response, Nathan decided to cut his hours of nightly sleep in half so that he could spend twice as much time working. He also ate only half as much food as usual in order to save money. He began running a small advertisement for his business in the local newspaper, but when the ad brought no response he began standing on the street corner passing out leaflets to advertise his goods and services. This didn't work, either. The creditors were knocking on Nathan's door. He was at his wits' end. Finally he sought out the great kabbalist Rabbi Yehuda Ashlag for advice.

Rabbi Ashlag listened to Nathan's story. Then he said, "You say you've tried everything. Do you really believe that's true?"

Nathan hesitated a moment. "Yes, I do believe it," he replied.

"Well," said the rabbi, "I'd like you to take a moment and really consider whether there's anything else you could possibly do in order to solve your problem. Really think about it as hard as you possibly can."

Nathan closed his eyes and thought as hard as he could. Was there anything else he might have done to solve his problems? Was there any stone he had left unturned? No, he concluded sadly. He had done everything, and nothing had worked. It was as simple as that.

He looked at Rabbi Ashlag and shook his head. "I honestly believe I've exhausted every possibility," Nathan said.

To his surprise, Rabbi Ashlag seemed anything but distressed. In fact, he smiled and said, "In that case, you have received a great gift. For now you can pray—really and truly pray from the bottom of your heart—for the Creator to come to your aid."

Why is it so difficult for people to ask for God's help? In contemporary society at least, the idea that we must solve our problems on our own seems to be built into our way of interacting with the world. Certainly this was not always the case. Throughout history even the most powerful leaders made a point of asking for divine help in their endeavors, and their stature was in no way diminished. But many people today don't really believe they need any intervention from outside the physical realm. Nor do they see any benefit to keeping their egos in check by asking for that intervention.

Each week at Kabbalah Centres around the world, during the third meal of Shabbat, we sing the Hebrew song *"Yedid Nefesh"*—"Beloved of My Soul." It's a beautiful song, but that's not the only reason we sing it. The lyrics of *"Yedid Nefesh"* remind us that we can't do it alone. We can't achieve our life's purpose on the sole strength of our egos. Learning that we need help can be a painful process, but as Rabbi Ashlag pointed out in the story above, it's also a great gift. There's something very liberating about taking the first step toward acknowledging our need for the Creator's help.

Ask for it

The next step is to ask for it. This tool is an acknowledgment of a power outside ourselves and a move away from a purely ego-based existence. But *asking* is more active than merely *needing*. Asking represents a more proactive step in our relationship with the Creator. This is not unlike the relationship between a

91

child and a loving parent. A very young child feels the need for help but only becomes capable of asking for it as growth begins to take place. We are like children who urgently need the help of our parent—and, more than anything, our parent desires all that's best for us. The more direct, the more personal, the more intimate our bond with the Creator becomes, the more promise it holds. Kabbalah teaches us to *walk with God every day,* a phrase derived from the first line of the Judaic Code of Law, which states, "Put God before you always."

This is not just a metaphor. The Creator truly is with us, from the moment we wake up in the morning until we fall asleep at night. Once we really take this idea to heart, we can begin to move closer to the full and equal partnership in creation that is such an essential principle of Kabbalah. Each of us has the potential to become that equal partner, and it was the Creator's plan from the beginning of time that we should realize that capability.

Partnership, moreover, includes the right to question, to intercede, and to influence decisions. As we transform, as we reveal the Light hidden within ourselves, our relationship with God matures and our influence grows. What begins as a simple parent–child relationship develops into a partnership in which we acquire all the rights and responsibilities that partnership demands. But it all begins with an acknowledgment that we're not alone and that it's a mistake to act as if we were.

Just as every great building has an architect, our world, too, has its master builder. A story from the Talmud illustrates this idea.

The Master Builder

An atheist once came to a great sage. He started telling him that he didn't believe in God. He wasn't sure what to believe in, but he couldn't believe some sort of "creator" made this world.

A few days later, the sage came to the man's home and brought him a beautiful painting. The atheist looked at the painting. He was in awe. It was the most exquisite painting the man had ever seen.

"This painting is so beautiful, who is the artist?" he demanded of the sage.

The sage answered, "Artist? What artist? No artist painted this. I just took a few colors, splashed them onto it, and what you see before you is the result."

The man began to laugh. "Surely you're joking. That's impossible! It's such a beautiful work of art, such exact curves, exact lines, beautiful colors. The correct mix could not have occurred just by you throwing the colors on the canvas. There must have been thought behind this magnificent work of art. There must have been premeditation. There must be an artist who planned this whole painting out, who created this work of art."

The great sage smiled, and he said to the atheist, "You can't believe this one work of art was created haphazardly and without thought, without a Creator. However, you want me to believe that this whole beautiful world with its oceans, forests, and trees, with its perfect seasons, you want me to believe that everything on this Earth came about without a Creator, without thought, without premeditation!"

When you believe it, you'll receive it

Each one of us literally has the power to change the world, because each one of us carries a spark of the Creator of the universe at the core of our being. In fact, the amount of Light that we reveal depends upon our understanding of the power we have to reveal it. With the Light, it's not a matter of *I'll believe it when I see it.* Instead, it's *When you believe it, you'll receive it.* This is a significant difference from our experience of the everyday world. If you walk into a dark room and flip on a light switch, the room will fill with exactly the same amount of light every time whether you understand the workings of electricity or not. In the spiritual realm, however, our *understanding* of an action's potential regulates the amount of Light that manifests itself. Our awareness and understanding of the power of our action are inseparable from the action itself. When we question our power to reveal the Light of the Creator, when we belittle our spiritual importance in the world, we activate a self-confirming prophecy.

It is never too late

As people begin to learn the principles of Kabbalah, they often feel that they have done too many bad things in their lives to be able to transform and bond with the Creator. In fact, this is what they *want* to believe. It frees them from accepting the need for positive change. It allows them to abdicate the responsibility for transformation, which is nothing less than the true purpose of our lives. Recognizing this process is one of Kabbalah's most profound psychological insights. It calls attention to the fact that apparent self-loathing is really just egotism with a reverse spin.

The spark of the Creator is always within us, and it is always pure. If you take a penny and hold it up in front of your eye in just the right way, you can easily block out the sun. But is the penny bigger or more powerful than the sun just because it can hide the sun's light? The penny does not extinguish the sun, but only conceals it. In the same way, our negative actions only conceal the Light within us—but we may begin to feel that the Light has gone out forever. No darkness that we bring upon ourselves, however, is greater than the Light of the Creator that is at our core. As long as we are alive, we have this divine Light within us, burning as brightly as on the day we were born. No matter how deeply hidden, the Light remains there waiting for us to reveal it. And it is *never* too late.

Higher than the angels, lower than the worms

Throughout creation, only humanity must *choose* to connect to the Light of the Creator. The sun, moon, stars, plants, and animals all behave exactly as it was ordained for them to act from the beginning of time. We alone have the free will to do exactly as we decide. If we are not 100 percent connected to the Light, it is because we have not chosen to be. If we disconnect from the Light of the Creator, if we decide to live in a self-serving, egotistical manner, we have the potential to sink below the worms. By the same token, we have also the power to rise even above the angels.

What separates us from the rest of creation is neither intelligence nor language nor the ability to use tools. We are the only creatures in the world who can select our own place in the hierarchy of creation. It lies within our power to choose transformation or not to choose it—to choose good with its rewards, or evil with its consequences.

A story told by the Baal Shem Tov very powerfully expresses Kabbalah's teachings concerning the Creator's judgment, and the nature of retribution for our transgressions.

The Hell Within

In a distant country there lived a man, Viktor, who was very angry with the way the kingdom was being ruled. One law after another came down from the king, one edict after another, yet no one had any knowledge of how these decrees were brought into being or what they were intended to accomplish. In fact, no one had ever seen the king. But there were suspicions that he spent every day in self-indulgent pleasure while his subjects struggled to live according to his ever-changing laws.

Finally Viktor decided to take action against what he perceived as this tyranny. Since he had no access to the king himself, there was a limit to what he could actually do, so he chose to set off a powerful bomb beneath a statue of the king as a way of making his feelings known.

It so happened, however, that several of the king's soldiers happened to witness this act of symbolic violence. When they reported what they had seen to the king, he immediately ordered Viktor's arrest. And although Viktor immediately denied blowing up the statue, he was handcuffed and brought to the king's palace. There he was placed in an empty room and left to await his fate.

Viktor was certain that he was going to be executed or imprisoned, but then a surprising thing happened. A guard appeared and said, "The king has ordered that you be given a job in the royal gardens. You can start working right away."

So Viktor was given a rake and a hoe, and he went to work in the king's gardens. It wasn't bad work. In fact, it was quite pleasant, especially since Viktor was given a small house and three good meals a day. Almost a year went by in this way. Then one day Viktor's work was interrupted by one of the guards.

"Do you still deny that you blew up the king's statue?" the guard asked.

"Yes, I do deny it," Viktor said, certain the good treatment he'd received was only intended to soften his resistance.

"In that case," the guard said, "the king has ordered that you be promoted. From now on you'll be working in the palace itself. This will mean more money, more authority, and more power. The king has ordered it."

So Viktor moved into the palace, where he became a supervisor of dozens of workers in all sorts of jobs. Yet he kept expecting that at any time things would change. He was sure that at some point he would be severely punished for blowing up the statue, especially if he confessed to it. But instead he kept receiving more promotions. Every few months a guard would appear and ask him if he had damaged the statue. Viktor would deny it, and then his situation would get even better. The fact was, he was now living much better than he had before his arrest.

The final step was the most incredible of all. Viktor was promoted to the king's innermost circle of advisors. Though he had once thought the king spent every day in hedonistic pursuits, he now saw the heavy responsibilities and difficult decisions that came with rulership. In fact, Viktor himself now played a major role in making those decisions. His ideas affected the entire kingdom—which, by the way, was just as discontented as ever. Sometimes he totally lost faith in the people he was helping to govern. Why couldn't they understand how hard it was to be a ruler? There were times when he felt tempted to simply turn the army loose on them—and then a strange realization came over him: this was exactly how he'd felt about the king before his arrest!

All the while, he still denied that he had placed the bomb at the statue. Though he now felt terribly guilty about doing such a thing, his denial had taken on a life of its own. Viktor felt that at this point he couldn't admit his deed even if he wanted to, not after he'd denied it for so long.

Then there came a day when Viktor found himself alone with the king. "I imagine you're surprised at the way things have been going since your arrest," the king said. "It hasn't been what you expected, has it?"

Viktor nodded. "Yes," he said, "it's been exactly the opposite of what I expected when I was arrested."

"But have you been happy here?" the king asked.

Viktor hesitated. On the one hand, his life had never been

better. He had greater material comforts than he could ever have imagined. But how did he really feel on the inside? The truth was, he had never felt worse. The more the king rewarded him, the more he felt burdened by what he had done. And now, in this very personal conversation with the king himself, it all seemed overwhelming.

Viktor burst into tears. "No," he said, "it's been horrible. I've never been more miserable, even when I had nothing. It's been hell!"

The king listened closely. "Yes," he said, "that's exactly what it's been. Because hell is not a physical location, whether in this world or the next. Hell is a an inner distance. It's an estrangement from the truth that grows greater as the truth becomes more clear. But just as the entrance to hell exists within our own hearts, so does the escape."

It was then that Viktor confessed his attack on the statue—and as soon as he did so, the pain that had come from his inner conflict vanished. The hell that had come into being in his heart was transformed into paradise.

Yet what had changed? Viktor had not emerged from some subterranean Hades, nor had he ascended into a celestial Heaven. The only change took place within.

From a kabbalistic perspective, this is a good story for several reasons. First, as an allegory, it presents a much more subtle interpretation of the Creator's justice than many people might expect. In addition, Kabbalah teaches that this is very much like the judgment that each of us will encounter when we leave the physical world. Despite their appearance for dramatic effect in folktales, Kabbalah does not seriously warn us to expect a stern tribunal or scales in which our good deeds are weighed against the bad. Indeed, any judgment rendered comes from ourselves alone—because at the end of our lives we are simply shown all that it was in our power to accomplish in the world. Our potential is displayed before us along with our actual achievement. We see what we *became* side by side with what we *could have become.*

Chaos and the meaning of angels

Over the past twenty years the topic of chaos theory has moved from the blackboards of theoretical physics to the language of popular culture. In particular, the so-called butterfly effect has captured our imagination. In simple terms, this principle states that in a sufficiently complex system, small-scale turbulence can amplify to produce very large-scale results. A butterfly flapping its wings in Beijing can eventually manifest itself as a tornado in Tulsa.

This is a powerful insight with great resonance in Kabbalah, but to really understand this principle we need to express it a bit differently. Chaos theory teaches that we can predict future events in complex circumstances only if we know everything that influences those circumstances, down to the smallest detail—and this is virtually impossible. Kabbalah also tells us that we may never know the ultimate results of our actions—or even of our thoughts—but that those results are certain to be much more powerful than we might ordinarily have expected.

Moreover, those results take place not only in the physical world, but also in the realms beyond.

A passage in the Zohar explains that we are like wonderful marionettes whose strings reach up to connect us to countless supernal worlds. But instead of these strings controlling us, *we* control the strings. Our actions in the world influence the spiritual worlds above us. A simple act of kindness allows more kindness to flow down into our level of experience—and this, in turn, empowers others to act kindly as well.

By describing our thoughts, feelings, and actions as connections to the spiritual realm, Kabbalah reveals the power of each and every human being to influence the world. Every action we take opens or closes celestial gates of courage and charity, mercy and love, and every other positive quality. Our actions directly control their manifestation in the world.

Indeed, the kabbalists tell us that these manifestations are nothing less than divine beings: angels in their own right. Like the subatomic particles described by modern physics, angels are concentrations of energy that are constantly flitting in and out of existence. We bring them into being by our deeds, our thoughts, and our feelings, and we can erase them in the same way. The positive angels that come about through righteous action work for our benefit, while negative angels hinder us on the path toward transformation.

While there are other and higher categories of angels in Kabbalah—including Michael, Raphael, and Gabriel, who appear before Abraham in chapter 18 of the Book of Genesis—the idea that we create our own angels is a basic kabbalistic teaching. These angels are not white-robed beings with wings and halos. They are the direct expression of what is in our hearts and minds. These angels fundamentally influence our experience of the world, and we ourselves bring them into being.

From this it follows that we must accept responsibility for whatever we encounter in the world, even those things that most distress us. Difficult as it may seem, we must realize that we ourselves are to some extent responsible for any and all suffering, no matter how remote it may seem from our lives. We must face the realization that if we had been better people, perhaps this might not have happened.

This must lead us to actually being better, starting immediately!

When they first discover this principle, many new students are amazed or even offended. They wonder how they can possibly be held accountable for evil things that are happening on the other side of the world, or even things that took place hundreds of years ago? As so often happens, this is putting the emphasis in the wrong place. Kabbalah does have answers to those questions. In the Zohar and its commentaries, there are detailed discussions of why everyday notions of time and space are not applicable in matters of spirituality. But the real point is this: It is best *for your own soul* if you accept responsibility for whatever you see, whether or not you can articulate a logical explanation for that responsibility. You will be closer to fulfillment if you think less about hows and whys and more about what you can do right now to reveal Light in the world. Your true purpose in life will be nearer to realization if you accept the idea that even a small act of kindness can amplify across the world and even across the boundaries of time itself. To use a phrase that comes up again and again in Kabbalah, *this is a spiritual law.* The law is operative regardless of whether we can understand or explain it.

A principle of quantum mechanics teaches that a single electron can exist in two places at the same time, even at opposite ends of the universe. A complex mathematical terminology has evolved to explain this, but who can do so in everyday terms? Yet the principle affects the state of our being at the most fundamental levels, independent of our acceptance or understanding of it, or even whether we know about it at all.

So it is with the power of our own actions and influences— and we should realize that we are recipients of influences as well. Our ability to live positively and proactively is dependent on the actions of others, perhaps in distant places, perhaps even in other times. In fact, our whole generation is built on the spiritual work that was done before. As we find our way on the path of transformation, we should give thanks to our predecessors for clearing the road.

Without the Creator we are less than nothing

Sometimes, when we've begun to understand our direct influence on the Upper Worlds, ego can reassert itself in new ways. We congratulate ourselves on the hard work we've done or the goodness we've brought into the world. But Kabbalah tells us that in order for the Light of the Creator to reveal itself in us and through us, we must have humility.

Without humility, we separate ourselves from others by placing ourselves above them. It's like shutting off a water main: no matter how many faucets you try to turn on in your house, nothing happens because the water has been closed off at its source. No matter how positive our actions might be, the absence of humility shuts down access to the Light and diminishes our ability to benefit ourselves or the world. Like water, the Light of the Creator always seeks the lowest level. When we raise ourselves above others, we lift ourselves out of the Light. And the higher we lift ourselves, the less Light is available to us.

According to kabbalistic teaching, humility is simply the understanding that nothing we have is ours. Our intelligence, our wealth, our beauty, even our spiritual greatness really belong to that part of ourselves that was hewn from the great mountain of the Creator.

Humility is the awareness that without the Creator we are literally less than nothing.

Ultimately, balance is the key. We need to be aware of our greatness, and we also need to recognize that the true source of our greatness resides in our connection to the Light.

Nipping negativity in the bud is much easier than dealing with it once it's become habitual. Often messages come to us for just this reason. These messages are like lifelines thrown to us by the Creator. By taking hold of them, we can rescue ourselves from negativity. Sometimes these lifelines are actual events taking place in our lives. On other occasions, they're intangible sensations of awakening that we feel within our soul. If we are alert enough to take advantage of these opportunities to extricate ourselves from negativity, we may be able to avoid other ways of getting our attention.

But even painful experiences have a positive spiritual intention, if only we're able to recognize it. That's the lesson of the following tale.

The Dark Angels, the Light Angels, and the Gray Angels

There was once a businessman named Joseph. He was having troubles in all areas of his life. His business was failing, his oldest son wanted to become a musician, and worst of all, he had very painful gout in his foot that none of the local doctors could treat. Unable to understand why all these terrible things were happening to him, he decided to ask the opinion of a great scholar and kabbalist who lived in the next town. The kabbalist's name was Rabbi Shalom Sharrabi.

During the journey to Rabbi Sharrabi's town, Joseph felt more miserable than ever—he couldn't sleep, his foot hurt, the carriage was cold and uncomfortable. But he was certain that if anyone could help him, it would have to be a person like Rabbi Sharrabi, who could see through the events of the everyday world to the hidden meanings within. As soon as the carriage stopped, the businessman went directly to Rabbi Sharrabi's house. There he was greeted by the rabbi's wife, who asked him to have a seat in the parlor. She told Joseph that the rabbi would be with him momentarily, gave him a glass of tea, and left the room. Joseph sat down in an overstuffed easy chair, which he found much more comfortable than the hard bench in the carriage in which he had just spent the last few hours. The easy chair was so comfortable, in fact, that he fell into a deep sleep. And he had a dream.

In his dream, Joseph was walking along a road that led into a small village. As he walked, a caravan of carriages and livery wagons and covered carts was passing by, all hurrying into a village up ahead. Joseph couldn't see who was riding in the carriages and wagons, but he saw that each vehicle had a sign painted on its side. The signs said things like "Prejudicial Speech" or "Cheating at Cards" " or "Shady Business Deals" or "Stretching the Truth." Joseph was intrigued by the signs, and he hurried to follow the wagons toward the village and into the village square. All the wagons and carriages that had passed him on the road were parked in the square, along with many more carts and carriages that seemed to have arrived earlier. In the center of the square was a large balancing scale.

All of this was a little bit odd, but not nearly as odd as what Joseph saw next. Stepping down from the wagons and getting out of the carriages was a crowd of otherworldly beings, whom Joseph immediately knew were Dark Angels. All of them were moving toward the scale.

Now Joseph became frightened, because he had heard that a Dark Angel was formed every time one acted in a negative manner. What's more, the signs on the wagons from which the Dark Angels descended suddenly looked terribly familiar to him. He realized that every sign on every carriage and cart represented things that he himself had done—not just once, but many times. He suddenly knew that every Dark Angel represented a negative act of his life, and that he was witnessing his own judgment. Every one of the angels was climbing onto one side of the scale.

"But surely I've done some good deeds in my life," Joseph thought to himself. "Why do I see only Dark Angels?"

Sure enough, more carts and carriages now entered the square, and they too had signs on them—signs that read "Feeding the Poor" or "Sincerity" or "Sharing with Friends" or "Giving to Strangers." And Joseph recognized these signs, too. With relief he now watched as the Light Angels—beings that had been formed by his own positive actions in the world— climbed down from the wagons and moved toward the opposite side of the scale. Gradually their weight began to counterbalance the negative presence. But not quite, for there were still many more Dark Angels than Light ones. Joseph was frantic. He knew his fate literally hung in the balance.

Now a few other wagons were coming into the square. These bore signs that read "Toothaches" and "Heartaches" and "Grief" and "Mourning" and "Gout"—and down from these wagons stepped Gray Angels. Joseph had never heard of Gray Angels, but he understood by the signs that they represented all the pain and suffering he had endured in his life. Still, he had no idea to which side of the scale they would lend their weight.

When they moved toward the Dark side, Joseph began to despair. But instead of climbing onto the Dark side of the scale, each Gray Angel grabbed one of the Dark Angels, pulled it off, and took it away. With each Dark Angel removed by the Gray Angels, the weight of the scale's positive side drew closer to balancing the negative, but Joseph could already see that there wouldn't be enough Gray Angels to remove all the Dark ones.

Worst of all, there weren't any more carts coming into the square. Frantic, Joseph looked toward the heavens and shouted, "Please! Send me some more pain and suffering!"

It was just at that moment that Rabbi Sharrabi's wife woke Joseph and told him that the rabbi could see him now. "Er, thank you, but that won't necessary, I'm feeling much better!" stammered Joseph. And he hurried back to his musician son, his failing business, and his gout.

In Kabbalah, the truth is rarely what it seems. In fact, the truth is frequently the opposite of what it seems, and the counterintuitive path is often the right one. Our reflexive desire to avoid obstacles and challenges, to say nothing of real hardship, works against our own best interests at the deepest levels of our being.

CHAPTER 6

The Twelve Spiritual Laws of the Way

For most of us, time lacks physical reality. It's not something we can see or hear or hold in our hands. Yet Kabbalah asks us to picture every minute, every hour, and every day as living things. Each day is given to us by the Creator in much the same way that children are given to their parents. Every day is a whole new world with a unique energy, like a newborn child. Like a child, each day has its own unique potential. What we can do today, we cannot do tomorrow. It's true that tomorrow we may be able to do great things, but we may not be able to do the great things that were scheduled for today.

1. Know that every day is an opportunity for transformation

Kabbalah teaches that every encounter with a new person is like entering a different universe. It's an opportunity to set ourselves free from the past and make a new beginning. In this sense, each new day is also like a living being. Every day is truly an opportunity for transformation.

When we understand this, it becomes clear that we should treat each day responsibly and with great care. Will we fill it with Light, using the day for sharing and spiritual work? Or will we fill it with negativity, selfishness, and darkness? Each day requires that we pay strict attention to our spiritual work, heeding its unique needs as well as the messages of wisdom that it is sure to bring.

2. Hear the Voice from Above

The concept of *Bat Kol* (Voice from Above) is very useful in this regard. *Bat Kol* is a gentle inner whisper that calls upon us to draw closer to the Creator. The call might be something as simple as a sudden urge to telephone an aging parent, or an impulse to volunteer your help at the homeless shelter that you pass on your way to work. Each day's *Bat Kol* is different, and each of us hears a different call.

Bat Kol is like a beacon of light that passes over us once a day. It does not appear in response to any wish, prayer, or positive action, but arrives as a no-strings-attached gift. It represents a great spiritual opportunity no matter where we are on the path to transformation. To hear this voice, we need only be conscious of and eager for its arrival, as though awaiting the visit of a close friend. When it comes, we need only to reach up and grab it. But without consciousness of *Bat Kol*'s existence and desire for its arrival, however, the beacon passes unseen and the opportunity is lost.

Here, as in many aspects of kabbalistic wisdom, understanding, awareness, desire, and intention are fully equal to positive actions in drawing us closer to the Light of the Creator.

3. Understand that we are all mirrors

Time and again over the course of our lives, we encounter negative events (and negative people) that may startle and upset us. It might be a traffic accident on the expressway, a news story on about an earthquake in Turkey, or a stranger at the supermarket suddenly enraged by a clerk's trivial mistake. Most of the time, when we see these things, our first inclinations are toward judgment and self-interest. We wonder who's at fault for the traffic accident, we rue the possibility of being late for work. We see the enraged man, wonder how he got so angry, and hurry toward the parking lot so as not to become involved. We experience these events as unfortunate coincidences, shreds from the patchwork fabric of modern life that we were unlucky enough to witness.

But Kabbalah teaches that *nothing* we see is a coincidence. Everything—particularly a negative event—has a reason and a purpose. Moreover, on the spiritual level everything we see is a mirror in which we ourselves are reflected. An angry stranger expresses something about our own anger and rage. A traffic accident reveals our insensitivity to the fragile nature of our own lives. The horror of the earthquake signifies a need for greater attention to our spiritual work, so that tragedy will no longer be a part of life.

Seeing negativity in the world is not an occasion for us to pass judgment, but a purposeful signal sent to us by the Creator so we may reconsider our path toward transformation. As Albert Einstein said, "God does not play dice with the universe." Just as what happens in our lives is what needs to happen, what we see in the world is what we need to face.

4. Trust in the Creator—*emunah*

The Rabbi and the Train

It was an insufferably hot day in the Odessa train station. An old rabbi patiently stood in a long queue to buy a ticket for a train trip. As he waited, one of his students happened by. "Where are you going, Rabbi?" the student asked. "To Kiev," the rabbi answered.

Hoping to save the rabbi from waiting in the heat, the student offered to take the rabbi's place in line while the rabbi took a seat in the much cooler and more hospitable waiting room. The rabbi accepted this kindness with gratitude.

When the student, after almost an hour, finally reached the

ticket window, he bought a ticket to Kiev and then went looking for his teacher. He handed the ticket to the old man, who thanked him and moved to board his train.

The student stopped him. "Excuse me, Rabbi, but . . . I paid for the ticket." "Yes," the rabbi replied, "thank you very much." Thinking that the old man misunderstood his intentions, the student now made it perfectly clear. "Rabbi, as you know I am very poor, I was hoping that you would reimburse me for the ticket." "But," the rabbi replied, "I don't have any money."

The student was shocked. "You were standing in line to buy a ticket to Kiev and you didn't have any money to buy one?" The rabbi nodded as though this was the most natural thing in the world. "I needed to go to Kiev but I didn't have any money, so standing in the line is the action I took. Then, thank God, God sent you to buy it for me."

"But now I don't have any money for a ticket," lamented the student, obviously very worried. "Well," said the rabbi, "let me suggest that you get in line." And with that, he turned and moved toward the train.

In every relationship, trust has to be earned. Step by step, trust is built from shared experiences over time—experiences that tell us when someone has our best interests at heart. We give people our trust today and tomorrow because they have been trustworthy in the past.

Our relationship with the Creator is no different. *Emunah,* or trust in the Creator, is not blind faith. It arises from an understanding of the spiritual laws, and from certainty that the Creator always intends what is best for us. *Emunah,* simply put, means embracing the principle that whatever happens is always for the best.

Clearly, this is a difficult step to take. If we are mugged on the street, our natural inclination is to be angry and upset—at the person who committed the crime, and at the Creator for allowing such a thing to happen. It may be hard to imagine a state of mind in which a mugging is seen as exactly what was needed at that precise moment. Yet for that rare person who trusts the Creator completely, this is precisely how the event would be viewed. As the Book of Job so eloquently puts it, "Though He slay me, yet I will trust in Him."

Though few of us have reached this level of *emunah*, it represents a degree of spiritual development toward which we all can aspire every day of our lives. The aspiration itself expresses a desire to trust, which Kabbalah recognizes as a first step toward the goal. Our task is to move toward the transformed state of being in which we trust the Creator completely and without hesitation.

Earlier we discussed how the amount of Light that we reveal in a particular action depends upon our understanding of the power we have to reveal that Light. The more we recognize our power to reveal the Light of the Creator, the more Light we reveal.

Now we will add a corollary to this spiritual law:

The deeper our trust in the Creator, the more power we have.

Emunah is beyond understanding in the everyday sense of the word. It involves much more than an intellectual grasp of the situation. It is more than just belief based on logical consideration of facts. Most of us, for example, have an *understanding* that if we act in a sharing way with someone, positive things will happen as a result of our action. The more we understand that our actions have positive effects in the world, the more possibility there is for a positive result. There is a cause-and-effect logic to this transaction.

Emunah, however, involves faith, and certainty that the effects of our positive actions extend beyond anything we can possibly understand. Understanding is an element of our trust and faith in the Creator, but we need to recognize that human understanding is limited. *Emunah* knows no limits. *Emunah* alone can make the sun stand still in the sky. *Emunah* alone can part the Red Sea.

Indeed, the parting of the Red Sea in the Book of Exodus is perhaps the most striking example of the power of trust. Just imagine the scene: the terrified children of Israel were trapped at the edge of the water, with the mighty Egyptian army bearing down on them from behind. Then Moses stretched out his arm and his staff. He called upon the waters to part, and what happened? According to kabbalistic teaching, nothing. Not a wave changed its course. Not a single drop of water receded. To bring about a miracle in the natural world, the people had to first create a miracle in their own hearts. In keeping with this, the Bible reports that when Moses told the Israelites, "Have no fear, and witness the deliverance God will work for you today," the Creator responded, "Why do you cry out to me? Tell the Israelites to go forward!"

This somewhat surprising command does not mean that the Creator was indifferent to his people's fate. Rather, it means that God has given us the spiritual tools to meet any challenge that presents itself—including the tool of absolute trust. But to benefit from that tool, we must act accordingly. The sages tell us that a single man, Nachshon, took it upon himself to enter the water, and he did so with total certainty. Still, he was soon engulfed up to his neck, and the Red Sea had not parted. A moment later he was choked by water pouring into his throat, and it was at this instant that the real miracle was accomplished. Even as Nachshon was about to drown, his trust never wavered, and a split second later the waters formed a wall up to the heavens. The inner condition of one man's soul was mirrored in the behavior of physical reality.

Like Nachshon, we must combine the power of trust with the power of deeds. Sometimes this can mean taking actions that might be described as counterintuitive, though few of us will be called upon to wade into the ocean. More often, the correct action is simply common sense, which should always be accompanied by higher awareness. If we're ill, we must seek medical attention, though Kabbalah tells us that it is the Light of the Creator that will cure us. The act of going to the doctor, together with our trust in the Light, culminates in healing. And the more trust we have, the less action is needed.

5. Ask for divine assistance

We are never alone in any challenging spiritual endeavor. Though transforming our desire to receive for the self alone is enormously difficult, the Creator is always there for us—returning our attention to the task, sending us lifelines, instruction, and inspiration. Still, there are times when the work of transformation seems beyond our capabilities. That's a good time to remember this biblical passage:

> *Open for Me an opening no more than the eye of a*
> *needle, and I will open for you supernal gates.*

We need only make a beginning in our spiritual work and the Light of the Creator will help us finish the job. As in the concept of *emunah*, the amount of work we need to do *before* the Creator steps in to help is very much dependent on the level of our spiritual development—and for most of us, a beginning means going to the limits of our ability. If there are ten rungs on a ladder, and all our efforts take us only to the ninth rung, the Creator will take us over the tenth. But help will come only after we have done our absolute best. Even if a task before us is blatantly beyond our abilities, we can be certain that the Creator understands our limits and will reward our best efforts with success.

6. Realize that we are always being tested

At every moment of our lives, there is a positive force drawing us toward the Light—toward sharing, toward transformation of our nature, toward lasting satisfaction and ultimate fulfillment, toward bonding with the Creator. And there is also a negative force pulling us toward the instant gratification and transitory pleasure of self-serving desire. In a sense, these two forces are at war. And our first job is recognizing that we are at the center of the battlefield.

If we blithely ignore the presence of the well-armed negative force, the chances of our survival are slim. If we are not vigilant, we risk the spiritual equivalent of being wounded or even destroyed. This vigilance in itself is a difficult task, since human beings are by nature a rather happy-go-lucky bunch. When things are going well, the everyday business of our lives somehow expands to take all our energy and attention. Are the children getting their homework done? Will the new refrigerator be delivered on time? Will we have a date next Saturday? The idea that a battle is taking place simply doesn't enter our minds.

Kabbalah urges us to be aware that we are always being tested—and that the tests become more challenging as we move closer to the Light.

The battlefield metaphor can be helpful here: If an enemy commander sees that our forces are strong, he will send more of his own troops into the struggle. When the positive side of our nature grows, the negative inclination also becomes stronger.

The Baal Shem Tov once spoke of a grand palace in which an exalted king resides. The closer we draw to the palace, the more guards are in evidence. The greatest number of guards, the strongest and the cleverest, surround the king's chamber itself. As we draw closer to the Creator, the most formidable guards appear to block our entrance. Not only is the task of transformation difficult from the beginning, but it becomes more difficult as we get close to the goal. In a way, this is a blessing. Though it's true that we must earn every inch of terrain on the spiritual battlefield, the opponent's strongest attacks come only when we've shown ourselves able to resist them. When the tests get harder, it's an indication that we are moving in the right direction.

Negativity is drawn to the Light of the Creator like a moth to a flame. The negative force always moves toward its opposite energy. If we don't attempt to reveal the Light, the negative side ignores us. But when we truly want to change, when we truly try to reveal more Light in the world, the negative inclination immediately comes to life.

There is no positive action that we can attempt, there is no act of sharing, kindness, charity, or repentance, that the negative side will not attempt to corrupt.

Doubt and confusion may appear in our most compassionate acts. We may berate ourselves for ever imagining that we could change our own nature, much less the world's. These doubts and questionings are negativity in action—telling us that we are reaching beyond our abilities, flying too high, wasting our time. The goal is to subvert any attempt toward spiritual growth. And the attack may be very well disguised. We may even imagine that it's our better judgment, or even our own conscience, speaking.

This inner doubt is one of the most powerful tools of the negative side of our nature. Doubt asserts itself in all areas of life, and certainly with regard to every topic in this book. It is one of the most spiritually destructive tendencies of human nature, since the Light we reveal depends on our understanding that we do indeed have the power to reveal Light. By subverting this understanding, doubt prevents us from gaining fulfillment for ourselves and others. "Who do you think you are? You can't change the world! No one person can make a difference! Things just keep getting worse and worse, and there's nothing you can do about it!" This is the rhetoric of doubt, and most of us hear it at a subliminal level throughout the day. Kabbalah cautions us to recognize it for what it is: the negative side trying desperately to prevent any positive action on our part. And the closer we come to really taking that action, the more doubts and questions are likely to rise to the surface. The good news is that this is often a sign that we're close to making real progress in our spiritual work. The bad news is that the doubts often succeed in preventing that progress from taking place.

> Rabbi Levi Yitzchak of Berdichov was a very righteous man. One day he happened to have a conversation with a very evil person. Rabbi Yitzchak considered the man and said, "I envy you." The evil man, knowing the rabbi's reputation, laughed, "Why would you possibly envy me?" And the rabbi replied, "Because if you change, you have more potential to reveal the Light of the Creator than I do."

The greater our desire to receive for the self alone, the more potential we have for revealing Light—because if we change, if we succeed in transforming our nature, our past negativity transforms as well. The more negative our actions have been, the more Light that comes to be revealed.

This is a central and somewhat complex principle of Kabbalah. Referring once again to the battlefield metaphor, we can not only defeat the negative forces, but we even have the power to turn their allegiance to the positive side. When we truly repent of our negativity, all the darkness for which we are responsible becomes Light. No darkness that we bring upon ourselves is greater than the Light of the Creator that is at our core.

The battle is raging. The enemy is clever and strong. But the fight can be won, and it is well worth winning.

7. Repent with joy

Everyone is responsible for destructive and negative actions— whether they're relatively trivial, as in speaking curtly to a business associate, or as serious as theft or infidelity. Under any and all circumstances, Kabbalah identifies repentance (*teshuvah* in Hebrew) as the proactive spiritual response. On the highway of life, repentance is our opportunity to make a complete U-turn. With true repentance, *any* negative action can be cleansed and transformed.

Repentance is a three-step process:

1. *Have true remorse.* Repentance begins with an understanding that we have done something wrong, and with regret for having done it. Here again, awareness and understanding precede action.

2. *Have certainty.* Out of this true remorse we gain the power to search our hearts until we can say with absolute certainty that we would never choose to repeat the negative act.

3. *Face the opportunity for negativity again, and make a different choice.* Once we are certain of ourselves, we must

proactively hope that the Creator presents us with a similar situation that will allow us to complete the process of repentance. We may actually long for that final test. Without it, we can never transform the negative act into a positive one.

Life almost never repeats itself in exactly the same way. The spouse who has been unfaithful during a business convention in Cleveland may never go to Cleveland again. More likely, a situation will arise that addresses the core of infidelity—that is, the breaking of trust. The connection between the original mistake and the opportunity to correct it will be concealed. The essence will be the same, but the appearance may be very different.

Clearly, repentance requires that we stay on our toes. True understanding is required to recognize the nature of our error when it is presented to us again.

Cleaning the Barn

Two boys worked for a scholar whom they respected very much. Both were given the task of cleaning an old barn that was to become their employer's study.

As you can imagine, the work of cleaning the barn was hard and dirty. The first boy was happy as he worked—whistling and singing as he accomplished his appointed tasks. The second boy did the work just as faithfully as the first, but not with nearly as much enthusiasm. He knew somebody had to do the cleaning; he just wished it wasn't him.

Finally, the second boy became fed up with the first boy's happiness. He stopped and asked, "Why are you so happy?"

The first boy thought about it for a moment and then replied, "I'm happy because I know that when we're done, our employer will have a clean room to sit in."

Though it is often difficult, repentance is a joyous process. It is the hard work we must do in order to create a resting place for the Light of the Creator. Through repentance we become better Vessels for the Light.

In repentance Kabbalah finds neither guilt nor sadness, both of which are expressions of the negative forces within us. They foster inactivity, self-involvement, self-loathing, and helplessness—each in its own way a form of desire to receive for the self alone. Worst of all, neither guilt nor sadness does anything to correct the act that caused them.

8. Be never satisfied

Rabbi Elimelech often told the following story to his students:

The Three Judges

When I pass on I will stand before the three judges of the heavenly court. They will decide if I am to enter Heaven, or be returned to life to complete my transformation.

The first will ask me, "Did you treat others with respect?" and I will answer, "Yes, but did I treat them with enough respect? No." And my answer will be written down.

The second judge will ask, "Did you study?" and I will reply, "Yes, I studied, but did I study as I was supposed to? No." And the answer will be written down.

Finally, the third judge will ask, "Did you love others as you loved yourself?" and I will answer, "Yes, but not completely." And this will be written down as well.

When there are no further questions, I will turn to leave the proceedings, headed, I am certain, for another incarnation in which I will try to do better. But the judges will cry, "Where do you think you're going? A person who speaks as much truth as you is needed in the Garden of Eden. Step this way."

Imagine yourself holding a lit candle in the middle of a darkened room. As it is the only light in the room, the candle seems fairly bright. Now imagine taking the candle outside in the sunlight. Though the candlelight is unchanged, its light seems diminished or even nonexistent. Only in the dark does the candle really seem to really make a difference.

As we move closer to the great Light of the Creator, and as we compare our Light to His, our spiritual accomplishments seem to diminish into insignificance. As we move farther from the Creator's Light, our accomplishments seem greater, and the more pleased with ourselves we become.

This is a spiritual law, but a rather paradoxical one that requires explanation. The phrase "pleased with ourselves" describes *contentment with our level of spiritual development.* This is something very different from the sense of genuine satisfaction and fulfillment that we experience in spiritual transformation. While our feelings of real fulfillment may increase, we may feel less and less satisfied with our *level* of spiritual achievements. Like great scholars or scientists, the more we accomplish, the more we become aware of what remains undone.

Even Moses repeatedly questioned his worthiness to perform the tasks God put before him. Yet we all know people who seem remarkably satisfied with their own self-importance, as if dazzled by the brilliance of their own candles. Kabbalah, however, explains that candles seem to grow brighter only as we move into darker territory. Self-satisfaction regarding spiritual growth is a clear sign that we are moving in a perilous direction.

I recently saw a highly successful movie star being interviewed on television. "Your life must be very hectic and exciting," said the interviewer. "Do you have time to keep up with what's going on in the world?"

The star looked puzzled. "I'm not sure I understand what you mean."

"Well, do you have time to read the newspaper? Do you watch the news on TV?"

Now the star shook his head and laughed. "No, I absolutely do not. But it's not a matter of time. I don't need all that negativity in my life. It's bad for my spiritual health."

As I watched this interview, it occurred to me that the spiritual health referred to by the movie star is not very different from the physical well-being of our bodies. In other words, what may be healthy for one person can be decidedly the opposite for another. If your life is filled with serious challenges, as is the case for many people in the world, it may really be wise to avoid exposure to unsettling images and information in the news or elsewhere. But a film star in Hollywood most likely has very different needs in this regard. What's bad for another person's spiritual health might be just what he needs.

Kabbalah teaches us to bring prosperity into our lives in every sense of the word, including the material sense. But Kabbalah also recognizes the danger of becoming complacent and self-satisfied.

There is something rather paradoxical about this. The Creator intends for us to be happy and fulfilled, and when we genuinely experience those feelings we should take joy in having fulfilled His intentions. On the other hand, if we are perfectly comfortable and without any sense of urgency in our lives, we can be sure that we have somehow left the spiritual path.

Unfortunately, leaving the path is an all too frequent phenomenon among people who begin spiritual work. Rabbi Ashlag, the great twentieth-century kabbalist, wrote that seeing this happen so often was one of the greatest disappointments of his life.

Remember: achieving fulfillment through spiritual transformation is not easy, nor is it supposed to be, but it is what you are meant to do. Learning to walk and to read are not easy either, but we accomplish those tasks in order to gain the rewards that they hold. We accomplish them because, barring some serious medical problem, it is not in our nature to spend our lives crawling around on all fours. When we fall down, we get back up again. But in our spiritual work, we may not even realize that we have fallen. That's why it's necessary to return again and again to kabbalistic tools and teachings.

A central purpose of Kabbalah is helping us to know the difference between real happiness and mere complacency or satiation. Without question, we should enjoy the good things in our lives. At the same time, we must always be aware that others' lives are less fulfilled than our own, and we must never cease trying to rectify that fact. We must never forget that all humanity is in the same boat. If some of us are sinking, all of us are sinking.

9. Walk like the blind

Kabbalah describes two categories of people on the path to transformation: those who are blind and know they are blind, and those who are blind and don't know it. People who know they are spiritually "in the dark" move through life with great care. They don't see as well as they would like to. Figuratively speaking, they get down on their hands and knees and crawl to make certain no danger lies ahead—and because they move with such great care, they're able to discover diamonds lying in their path.

The rest of us imagine that we see everything. Because of this, we find ourselves constantly falling into the spiritual equivalent of snares, traps, and pitfalls. Even worse, we overlook the jewels—the opportunities for transformation—spread out before us. We see the world through a lens of ego that severely distorts the terrain. We misread signs. We take the wrong road. We're a danger to ourselves and to those around us.

The wisdom of Kabbalah teaches that regardless of our level

of spiritual development, it is best to think of ourselves as spiritually blind and to assume that our understanding is very limited. This in itself is not an easy task. It's a challenge for those of us who have studied a bit of Kabbalah and are suddenly euphoric about a new whole way of looking at the world. But it's even more difficult for those of us who have studied a great deal and think we know exactly how the system works. The fact is, the more we really know about transformation, the less likely we'll believe that our spiritual vision is 20/20.

True spiritual growth is complicated. We need perseverance, courage, and determination. As we draw closer to the Light of the Creator, the journey becomes more complex—and at the same time, more Light is revealed by our efforts.

10. Use death as a motivation

It's been said that human beings are unique in our awareness of the inevitability of death. But if we honestly examine our behavior, we must ask whether we're really aware *enough*. If we are in fact the only animal with the ability to be conscious of our own death, most of us don't take advantage of that ability.

The term *near-death experience* has become familiar in recent years. It refers to characteristic visions and sensations that have been experienced by some accident victims, or by patients who were clinically dead for a period of time during surgery. Almost always, these visions have included the presence of a great Light and an awareness of a completely loving and benevolent power. How would your life change if you were to undergo a near-death experience? Would you spend less time on your own needs? Would you give more attention to emulating the loving energy you discovered in your vision?

Perhaps. But why should it require a car accident or open heart surgery to move you in this direction? Those events are certainly dramatic, but afterward you would still be living in the same world you're in right now, faced with the same hopes and fears. Perhaps the only thing that would really change as a result of a near-death experience would be your *awareness*— your consciousness of the brief amount of time you've been given and the importance of how you use that time.

Kabbalah reminds us that we are having a near-death experience all the time.

No matter where we are on life's road, death stands at the end of it until the world's transformation is complete. We must understand that we exist for only a brief instant. It's simply a fact of this phase of creation.

Kabbalah teaches us to use death as a motivation for focusing our lives on what really matters. As a spiritual tool, we may even envision our own death in order to grasp the limited time we have for accomplishing our task. Without this awareness of our limits, it's our nature to turn away from our true best interests. We can therefore use death against itself. When the process of transformation is complete, death will disappear from the world.

11. Experience the pain as our own

More than just noticing the pain that people experience in the world, we must *actively search for it and teach ourselves to experience it as our own.* To accomplish our spiritual work, we have to get our hands dirty. But this is not just an exercise in sadness or guilt. The true purpose of feeling others' pain is to inspire us to attend to our spiritual work, which includes taking physical action in the world to alleviate the human suffering.

A kabbalistic teaching makes this point very powerfully. If everything in the world has a place and a purpose, the sages asked, what is the purpose of atheism? When should we put aside our belief in and devotion to God? The answer is: whenever we see someone in pain. At that moment even our connection to the Creator should be put aside in favor of practical action to help another human being.

In discussing this with Kabbalah students, I've sometimes seen them shake their heads sadly. "It sounds very inspiring," they tell me, "but what's the use? The magnitude of suffering in the world is just too great. There's just too much pain for anyone to really make a difference." This line of thinking is one of the most potent weapons of our negative inclination. Kabbalah emphatically counsels us not to measure righteousness "by volume." Just as the perturbations from a butterfly's wings can eventually create a tornado, every positive act, however small, brings Light into the world, which opens a channel for more Light—and in this way the transformation of mankind will eventually become a reality.

Suppose your house were on fire and you had time to save some of your possessions, but not all of them. Would you throw up your hands and say, "Forget it! If I can't save it all, I'll just let it burn."? Or would you run into the house and grab what you could? Most of us would do the latter, and the same principle applies to the situation of the world in general. Alone, we cannot possibly alleviate all the pain and suffering that exist. But this is not a reason to stop trying. Kabbalah tells us that if we can help even one person, it is as though we've saved the whole world.

12. Don't judge others

Kabbalah implores us to judge ourselves and our motivations with great care. One of our obstacles on our spiritual path, however, is the tendency to become judgmental about other people. This is especially true at the beginning of the journey: We've learned a little about the spiritual laws, and suddenly we think we know exactly what's wrong with everybody else. Even worse, we may make the mistake of telling them!

The focus of our judgment should always be on ourselves, never on others. Regardless of our level of spiritual development, our understanding of the spiritual laws and their effects in the world is limited. Thinking that we know how everything works in the spiritual world is a certain indication that we know very little indeed. Full awareness of our own intentions and motives is hard enough, so how can we pass judgment on another person's life? Moreover, the spiritual foundations for a person's troubles are complicated and often obscure. If we accept that our understanding of the spiritual world is limited, it is foolish to imagine that we can see through the intricacies of the spiritual universe enough to penetrate the mysteries of other people's destinies.

Imagine that a close friend has suddenly been stricken by a severe illness. Clearly, he is suffering—and according to Kabbalah, we are all ultimately responsible for our own pain. Should we then tell our friend that his predicament is his own responsibility? On the spiritual level, this may be true—but the more real question is, What good does this judgment do? How will it benefit him, in the midst of his suffering, to hear that he is responsible for it? Passing judgment on the spiritual causes of others' distress brings neither them nor us closer to transformation.

Instead, our first responsibility should be not to judge but to lend assistance. A person in pain needs relief, not moral reflection. A homeless man needs shelter, not philosophy, however well informed it might be. Unless we are certain that our judgment will help another person toward transformation, it is best to say nothing and to take positive action toward relieving the immediate distress. Often, the simple act of *nonjudgmental* listening is the best thing we can do for anyone.

The whole purpose of spirituality is to become *more* conscious of the needs of others, *more* sympathetic, and *more* caring. So beware of the road that leads you in the other direction—toward judging others harshly. This is not a true spiritual path.

PART THREE

Spiritual Transformation

CHAPTER 7

Understanding Our Thoughts and Feelings

Living as a spiritual person doesn't mean letting go of the thoughts and feelings that fill your life every day. There's no need to "purge" happiness, love, fear, desire, exhilaration, or even anger in order to follow a truly spiritual path. In fact, the opposite is true, and our emotions can be hugely helpful in connecting to the Light. But we do need to ask one very basic question: Are we in control of our emotions, or are our emotions in control of us?

Kabbalah provides a detailed description of the role of human feelings in the structure of the spiritual world.

Our emotions are connected to specific frequencies, or emanations, through which the Light of the Creator radiates from the Upper Worlds. Each of these emanations has a name and a precise purpose. They are like a portal through which energy flows between the physical and the spiritual dimensions. How we feel and, more importantly, the intention and motivation underlying our feelings affect the rate and quality of the flow.

Here is the fundamental question we must ask ourselves: Are our emotions manifestations of our desire to receive for ourselves alone, or do they express our desire for the purpose of sharing? We are given our emotions to assist us in our spiritual work, but the choice to use them for that purpose (or not to use them) always remains our own.

Live with joy

The sixteenth-century kabbalist Rabbi Isaac Luria was one of the great spiritual lights in the world. It is said that angels appeared when he prayed. Rabbi Luria himself attributed his great gifts to one simple quality: he lived every day with joy. Indeed, Kabbalah teaches that the Light revealed by any action is proportional to our joy in performing the act. Conversely, in the absence of joy, even great acts of sharing and kindness are severely diminished. The good we are able to do in the world is limited when we are not happy in our spiritual work.

When an otherwise positive act is performed with a joyless heart, it's as if a blanket has been thrown over a burning light-bulb. The bulb may be illuminated, but the covering prevents the light from illuminating the room—and the light might as well not be burning at all. Similarly, joy arising from unworthy motives also restricts the flow of Light. Burglars may feel tremendous joy when they've successfully robbed a home, but this is only happiness at the gratification of a self-serving desire. And Kabbalah teaches that when an emotion is exploited by our desire to receive for the self alone, the source of that emotion in the spiritual dimension shuts down. Our capacity to experience that emotion, for good or bad, is weakened and eventually disappears altogether.

If a child is given a toy hammer and uses it to build something, his parents let him keep it. If he uses it to pound on his baby brother's head, his parents take it away. The tool remains the same. The difference is in how the tool is used. When our emotions serve the desire to receive for the self alone, it is as though the Creator says, "Well, if you're going to use it *that* way, you can't use it at all anymore."

Appreciation brings joy

A man went to a doctor, who told him that he had a fatal illness. The man was devastated. He left the doctor's office and wandered the streets, depressed and in shock. Several hours later, the doctor called him back to tell him that a mistake had been made. It turned out the man was not sick at all—he was as healthy as could be. The man was overjoyed. He again wandered through the streets, but now he felt as if he was walking on air.

What changed between the time the man was mistakenly told he was dying and the discovery that he was healthy? What prompted his emotional roller-coaster ride? It certainly wasn't the state of his health, which remained the same throughout.

The change was the man's appreciation for his health. Once the apparent danger had passed, the man had a renewed awareness of the gift of health that he had always taken for granted. It was as though health had been given to him anew. His appreciation brought him joy.

This can happen on any scale of experience. As a young man, the nineteenth-century Russian novelist Fyodor Dostoyevsky found himself sentenced to death along with some other prisoners on a trumped-up political charge. The experience was recounted in several of his novels. As the troops of the firing squad loaded their guns, the young writer realized that he had about five minutes to live. Strangely, this seemed to him like an extremely long period of time. There was something positively luxurious about how long it was. Dostoyevsky realized that he could spend an entire minute staring at the sunlight reflecting on the dome of a church in the distance, and he would still have four minutes left over. It seemed like an eternity.

Then, suddenly and astonishingly, the execution was called off. It had been a trick to frighten the prisoners into submission. Rather than being joyful, Dostoyevsky was struck by a sense of loss. He felt the intensity he'd discovered in each moment slipping away. Why couldn't he recapture it? Why couldn't he live his whole life with the sense that each instant was a perfect jewel? Try as he might, it seemed to be impossible.

We can face similar dilemmas even in more everyday circumstances. Once I was praying in the synagogue when some noise started in a hallway outside. At first I found it very annoying—but what was that annoyance really based upon? I felt empowered to waste my time in misery because I was certain there would be more time where that came from. But what if there was no more time? If this had been my last moment on earth, that commotion in the hallway might have been the most precious sound imaginable. If I were a person who had no home or no friends, just being inside the synagogue among other people would have been a deeply cherished experience.

Nothing we have is inherently ours. Everything is given to us, and transformation means learning to appreciate these gifts. This includes not only material goods, but also the qualities of our body, mind, and spirit.

Kabbalah teaches, for example, that both our eyesight and our powers of spiritual insight are miraculous gifts that do not belong to us. They are two of the many tools that have come into our possession as tools for transforming our nature—and each tool offers us its unique capability for doing good in the world. We should take joy both in the gift of these tools and in the positive actions they help us perform.

Realize that envy is a constant temptation

Envy is the mirror image of joy. Just as joy is linked to appreciation for what the Creator has given us, envy is *lack* of appreciation. It's a self-destructive longing to be another person—to have someone else's life or some aspect of it—with an implicit rejection of who we really are.

We've seen how *emunah*, trust in the Creator, is a deep certainty that God intends what's best for us. This divine intention is present in everything we do or that's done to us. This is an absolutely fundamental kabbalistic idea, as is this logical extension of it: *We always receive exactly what we deserve and need.*

Envy, then, is a failure to trust in the Creator's wisdom. It's a way of telling God, "You don't know what's best for me, or maybe you just don't care. If you did, you would give me what that other person has, not what I'm stuck with." Think of your life as a car traveling down a highway. The Creator drives the car, but when we are envious of another person's possessions, fame, or power, we are saying we don't like the Creator's driving. No one likes a backseat driver. If we express this feeling enough, the Creator says, "If you're so smart, you drive," and hands over the wheel. Fasten your seat belts!

By not appreciating what we have, we may lose it. When we chase after what isn't ours, we are in danger of what has been given to us. Covet your neighbor's house, in other words, and the smaller house that has served you so well may end up in ruins. And more than that's in jeopardy: your health, your family, and even your life are only on loan to you. Failure to trust the Creator's plan in any particular endangers the plan as a whole. By focusing our attention on what we don't have, we endanger the good things in our lives right now, as well as those that await us in the future.

With this in mind, we should make a distinction between envy and a desire for positive change and spiritual growth. All of us know people we admire, people whose achievements embody our own aspirations. Visiting a museum, a young artist may admire the work of a master—or a newcomer to spirituality may hunger to emulate the life of a righteous person. What distinguishes these desires from jealousy or envy is the intention that underlies them. If the goal of an artist or a spiritual seeker is connecting to the Light of the Creator through their own work, the intention is thoroughly positive. But if the objective is fame or power for themselves alone, the difference in intention is more significant than anything in either the quality of the paintings or the time spent in prayer and study.

Envy is a constant temptation, perhaps more so in the contemporary world than at any other time in history. Over the millennia, most people lived their lives in resignation to what fate had brought. If you were born poor, as the vast majority of people were, it was virtually inconceivable that you would ever become rich. Today, at least in North America, we have infinitely greater opportunities. But we must also deal with the negative feelings that arise when those opportunities aren't realized as quickly as we want—or worse, when others have fulfilled their opportunities and we haven't. In this circumstance, we may find ourselves thinking reactively: "Why haven't I got what they've got? It's not fair!" In contrast, a proactive response asks, "What can I do, starting now, that will make me deserving of the things I desire in life?"

It's not easy to respond this way. It does become easier, however, if you remember that it's not about being a saint; it's in your own self-interest to live your life proactively and with a desire for connection with the Light of the Creator. The more we aspire to reveal the Light through the completion of our spiritual work, the more likely it is that our desires will be fulfilled.

We must keep our intentions pure. Yearning for the Light is a feeling given to us to assist in our spiritual transformation. Jealousy and envy are distortions of this feeling and represent a corruption of the flow of energy from the Upper Worlds. And Kabbalah teaches that there is nothing that the negative inclination will not seek to corrupt.

Know all the meanings of fear

Although it's an emotion we naturally try to avoid, fear has a distinctly positive side. If we had no fear—of falling, of fire, of rattlesnakes—we probably wouldn't be here today. In a sense, fear keeps us alive in a physical world that contains many dangers. The spiritual world has its dangers also. At one time or another, all of us have contemplated a spiritually reckless act such as dishonesty, disloyalty, or perhaps even theft. Suddenly we were overcome by a sensation very much like fear that helped us back off from taking the leap. Kabbalah teaches that what we do, and even what we think, has an influence not only on those around us but even on the entire world. This creates a healthy fear, that is, a reluctance to do something that will have a harmful effect.

In fact, there are many healthy forms of fear, such as when someone says, "I have a healthy fear of the ocean," or "I have a healthy fear of power tools." Such fears keep us attentive. Without paralyzing us, they demonstrate our respect for real peril. Kabbalah tells us that these sorts of fears are messages from a benevolent Creator, sent to assist us in preserving our physical and spiritual well-being. Most often, a painful sense of impending danger means that there actually *is* possible danger ahead and that we'd better change our course.

Fear that immobilizes us is another matter. Action, as we've discussed, is an essential part of Kabbalah. Transformation can't take place if we're trapped in a corner, whether it's physically, emotionally, or spiritually. While there's no denying that change can be frightening, here as in every other area of our spiritual work we need to accept the challenge and push ourselves as hard as we can. For many people, this means overcoming fears of many kinds, including the fear that we may never reach the goal. For others, the paralyzing fear may manifest in an extremely tangible way. It can take the form of a phobia— whether of closed spaces, open spaces, spiders, or a thousand other possibilities.

From a kabbalistic perspective, the key is to recognize the common origin of all immobilizing fears, whether their point of reference is in the physical world or in our hearts and minds.

We are truly not alone

At its worst, fear creates a "circle the wagons" state of mind that closes us off from the rest of the world, and from the Light of the Creator as well. Rather than turning in on ourselves, we must open ourselves to others and to God. We must recognize that we are not alone—that when we truly confront our fears, the Creator will help us.

In light of this notion of a truly helping God, how can we

explain the emphasis the Bible seems to place on "fear" of God, or the virtue of people who are described as "God-fearing"? To a large extent, I believe this is a problem of translation. "Awe" is a word that much more accurately conveys the meaning and intention of the biblical text. This denotes a heightened sense of respect that inwardly motivates us to spiritually correct behavior. It has nothing to do with a fear of physical punishment. It is unrelated to the prospect of being condemned to an eternal hell of fire and brimstone, although this doleful vision has for centuries been employed to terrify humanity.

When we are in the presence of someone we deeply respect—whether it's a parent, friend, or colleague—our desire to fulfill their expectations of us certainly does not depend on the possibility that they might do us physical harm. On the contrary, our awareness of their love and respect is what really influences us. In the same way, when we put God "before us always," as the Bible says, we internalize the knowledge that the Creator is always aware of our actions, and we naturally behave in accordance with that knowledge. If that involves fear, it's only fear of not fulfilling our potential as beings of the Light.

Always be aware of anger

Sometimes it breaks over us like a huge slow-moving wave, and on other occasions it strikes as suddenly as lightning. The cause may be obscure or all too obvious: someone says the wrong thing, or says nothing, or says the right thing at the wrong time. In an instant we're red-faced, unable to speak, perhaps close to violence. Doors are slammed and dishes broken. Overcome, we not only forget who we are, but literally become someone else. Anger turns Dr. Jekyll into Mr. Hyde.

Anger causes a complete and instant disconnection from the Light. Darkness descends—and Kabbalah tells us that this is because anger is fundamentally ego-driven. Whatever the specific circumstances, we're convinced that we've received some pain or insult we didn't deserve. And since ego denies the active presence of the Creator in the events of our life, we react with anger. In the hierarchy of offenses against the Creator, the Zohar places anger right up there with idol worship. We are ready to sacrifice everything to the false god, the Golden Calf that we ourselves have created.

Kabbalah tells us that anger has its source in the same emanation of Light as judgment. But with its attributes of control, balance, and mercy, judgment expresses an intention to restore stability. Anger, on the other hand, is an instrument of chaos. It connects us to nothing but our own destructive instincts. It cuts us adrift.

Awareness of the consequences can be a powerful first line of defense against ego-based anger. If we understand that by giving in to anger we are about to completely disconnect from the Light, we are more prepared to deny the ego and soften our judgments with mercy. At the same time, Kabbalah teaches us to recognize the source of the anger as a messenger of the Creator, whose motives are always in our best interest. All it takes is an instant of clear awareness for us to move beyond purely reactive responses to provocation. Then we can take control of negativity before it becomes unmanageable.

All this, of course, was already known thousands of years ago. As it is written:

> *He who is slow to anger is better than a strong man,*
> *and a master of his passions is better than the*
> *conqueror of a city.*

Embrace love

Love is one of humanity's favorite topics. *Bartlett's Familiar Quotations* lists no fewer than a thousand entries under the heading of *love*. It's the subject of countless books, psychology papers, poems, and astrological forecasts. There's romantic love, love of nature, brotherly love, parental love, physical love, and spiritual love. But although love takes many forms, Kabbalah sees all of them as derived from the same emanation in the spiritual realm. The many kinds of love are all defined by whether we use them to reveal and share the Light of the Creator, or whether their Light is only ensnared and exploited by selfish desire.

In a relationship where two people truly place their partner's needs ahead of their own, for example, we presage the deep and enduring fulfillment that will be realized when the world completes its transformation. In that final stage of Creation, we will reunite with the Creator and receive all the blessings of the Light. This is our goal and purpose in the world, and love also holds this potential when it is focused in the proper way. Holy matrimony is indeed whole because it is here that *two people become one.*

Unfortunately, we don't always experience love just this way. More often than not, what we call love becomes centered on the good feelings that we *receive* from another person. Clearly, receiving is a part of even the best relationship, but problems begin when we allow getting to take precedence over giving. This self-focused love places our needs ahead of others'. We are more likely to ask, "What am I getting?" than the infinitely more important "What am I giving?"

Moreover, ego-based love tends to idealize its object and obscure the object's true identity. As a result, the objects of our love become almost interchangeable, as the real person is subsumed within a fantasy of our own reflection. The individual human being literally disappears and is replaced in our eyes by our own needs, desires, and passions. We love who we *want* the other person to be rather than for what he or she actually *is*. Self-focused love renders us as blind to their individuality as we are to their needs. It is a love driven by the desire to receive for the self alone.

Self-centered love cannot last, for the simple reason that it's based on qualities that also can't last—for example, the way someone looks, or the prestige of their career, or the amount of money they have in the bank. Under these circumstances, love can survive only as long as the material foundation remains intact. We need to emphasize again that when an emotion is exploited by our desire to receive for the self alone, the source of that emotion in the Upper Worlds is cut off. The misuse of love threatens us with the loss of love in all aspects. Like with a mischievous child, something we want very badly must be taken away until we can learn how to use it properly.

In love, as in all things, Kabbalah asks us to place the focus on giving rather than getting. But as human beings, this is not our natural inclination. True love, like the process of transformation itself, requires us to go out of ourselves, to go beyond our inborn need to receive, and to place the needs of others ahead of our own. By turning away from our natural inclination, we move ever closer to the nature of the Creator. We come to an awareness that *all true love is the love of God*.

CHAPTER 8

Using the Spiritual Tools

Earlier in this book we emphasized the need for God's help in bringing about our transformation, and the importance of acknowledging that need. Once this is understood, we also need to recognize the many tools that the Creator has provided to help us accomplish our spiritual work. On the simplest level, we have our physical bodies, our intellect, and our emotions. Like hand tools, these have the great advantage of familiarity and ease of operation. They also have the disadvantage of being so familiar to us that we overlook their true purpose of revealing the Light.

The Creator has also provided us with what could be called *spiritual power tools*. These can help us complete our work more quickly, but they're also a bit more difficult to operate. There are many of these power tools, and we will provide the major ones here.

The tools you select, and how you use them, are your choice. But remember: transformation is the core concept of Kabbalah, and the purpose of any tool—including this book—is to help you transform self-serving desire into desire for the purpose of sharing. That's what it's all about. Whether we use five tools or five hundred to reach this goal is immaterial. Whether we walk or take an airliner, the destination is the same.

Still, finding the tool that works for us can make a difficult journey a little easier.

Share

Our Inner Nature

A great sage who was a very close advisor to a powerful king had an argument one day with some of the king's other advisors. He felt that it was not possible to change the nature of an animal, whereas the others thought that it was possible, through practice and teaching. And they decided that they were going to prove this to him by training an animal.

A few months later, they sat down with the sage before the king, and at the clap of their hands a cat came in, carrying trays of food. It carried the food onto the tables. After they had finished the first course, it removed their dishes, and throughout the whole meal acted as a human waiter.

At this point they were sure that they had finally proven the sage wrong. "See," they said, "you can change the nature of an animal."

The sage then reached into his bag and pulled out a small box. He opened the box, and out jumped a mouse. The cat dropped all the dishes and all the trays, and started running after the mouse.

Smiling, the sage looked at the other advisors and said, "You can make a cat or any other animal act differently, but you cannot change the internal nature of a cat or any other animal."

Now, a human is not like any other animal. Yes, it *is* very difficult to change his nature—difficult, but possible. This is something we must realize if we really want to achieve our life's purpose. We have to go against our nature to become like the Creator, to change our desire to receive for the self alone to the desire to share. We must change that desire internally. It is not enough to act in a sharing way. We must change our essential nature that underlies our actions.

The single most effective tool for bringing us closer to the Creator is an act of true sharing—and true sharing takes place when we put another's needs ahead of our own. It is a very simple idea, yet extremely difficult to accomplish. In fact, it is really as close as we can come to making our own nature one and the same with God's. But difficult as it is, this is what we are really meant to do, and what we really want to do at the deepest level of our being. To begin liberating our desire to share, each act of true sharing must penetrate the armor of our desire to receive for the self alone.

Imagine for a moment a world in which people considered the hopes and fears of other people before they thought about their own needs—and if they did this without material benefit or heavenly reward, but for its own sake, for the sheer joy of doing it. War between nations, hatred between individuals, deep-seated bigotry, and petty animosities simply could not exist in such a world. Placing the needs of others ahead of our own would eliminate the reasons for corruption, bigotry, jealousy, and all forms of human misery. And this could be accomplished without any reference to God, religion, or spirituality.

True sharing is a panacea, a genuine cure-all for the spiritual malaise that afflicts so much of mankind. But why, if its benefits are so great, do people find it so difficult to make this change in themselves, or even to consider making it? Why, despite the teachings of Kabbalah and many other spiritual traditions, is it so hard to love our neighbors as ourselves?

Answering this question requires an understanding of two points. First, although sharing is woven into the fabric of our being at its core, it is *against our nature* at the level of everyday experience. The human body is a pure expression of desire to receive for the self alone. The body does not eat, sleep, or reproduce for the benefit of others; these are the things that it really wants to do—self-interest pure and simple.

In kabbalistic terms, real sharing must by definition be counterintuitive: it must go against the reflexive urges of our human nature.

When a mother feeds her child, for example, she is certainly sharing in the sense that food is passing from her hand into the baby's mouth. At the emotional level, too, feelings of love and caring pass from her heart to the child's. But—and for many new students, this is a very difficult notion to grasp—this is not sharing of the kind that the sages of Kabbalah describe. A mother nurturing her child is a beautiful thing, but it does not represent transcendence of self-serving desire. It is a *confluence of interests* rather than a core transformation of our nature. Cold-hearted as this may sound, it is a very fundamental distinction. Real sharing, like electricity, generates Light by passing through resistance. This is the quality that makes it so difficult to accomplish, as well as so powerful when it really is achieved.

A second reason for the scarcity of true sharing is the competition that it faces. The Creator's presence, as Kabbalah teaches, manifests itself in the universe as Light. But what kind of Light is this? Is it the neon kaleidoscope of downtown Las Vegas, or the overwhelming brightness of a nuclear detonation? On the contrary, Kabbalah compares the Light of the Creator to a gently burning candle. In order to truly understand and appreciate the Light, we must also realize that it can't compete with the pure rush of transitory pleasures and material indulgences. It's an odd but seemingly universal principle that what's best for us is often initially less attractive than what isn't. Few children would rather drink carrot juice than sugary soda drinks. Many more people read supermarket tabloids than great works of literature, or even good newspapers. The seductive attractions of the material world can be compared to the bright flash of light that accompanies a short-lived bulb: for a split second, it's hundreds of times brighter than a single candle. Lighting the house of your life with short-lived bulbs, however, can become quite tiring, not to mention expensive, yet this is what many people choose to do. They think their world is being lit up by that sudden flash, when in fact they themselves are being blinded by it. This blindness is what causes the vast majority of humanity to trade the authentic fulfillment of sharing for superficially exciting substitutes. This is not to say that life shouldn't be entertaining and fun. But Kabbalah teaches that our truest and deepest interests lie in aspiring toward something more. In order to see the candle, we've got to stop short-circuiting the lightbulbs for a moment—and when we see how good that feels at the soul level, we may stop short-circuiting them once and for all.

If you forget every other thought in this book, bear this one idea in mind:

All by itself, true sharing can transform the world. This refers not only to the sharing of physical objects, but especially to the sharing of wisdom and the Creator's Light.

SHARING IN ACTION

1. Be before doing

Sharing, first and foremost, is an inner quality of being. Only when this has been achieved can action in the real world express the true desire to share. The foundation of sharing is not the transfer of objects from one owner to another, but the decision to live as a person who aspires to make his or her nature one with that of the Creator. Sharing, therefore, is not charity, which is a separate and distinct spiritual tool. A sharing person makes a deep commitment to connect with the Light, whose very nature is to give of itself. At the same time, he or she makes an equally strong commitment to restrict and resist the antithesis of the Light's nature, which is the desire to receive for the self alone. Finally, a sharing person diligently uses the tools of Kabbalah to strengthen and sustain those intentions.

The first step, therefore, is to make this three-part resolution:

- to connect with the Light;
- to restrict self-serving desire; and
- to use the spiritual tools of Kabbalah.

When you're ready, undertake that commitment with the utmost seriousness. Everything else flows from that decision.

2. Be ruthless and without mercy

These are not qualities that are ordinarily celebrated in books on spiritual development. But Kabbalah implores us to ruthlessly seek out selfish desire wherever it may be hidden in our souls, and to make ourselves totally unforgiving of it. These are essential qualities of a sharing person.

How can you teach yourself to hunt down the desire to receive for the self alone, which is often extremely well camouflaged? Kabbalah offers some very practical guidelines. Whenever a feeling seems overwhelming, whenever a desire feels utterly irresistible, whenever saying "Stop!" or "No!" seems wholly impossible, you can be almost certain it's an expression of the negative side of our nature. Remember: the Light is a candle, not the flash of a firecracker. The truth is never strident, and it can easily be drowned out, at least for a while.

Right now, are there influences in your life that seem powerful beyond question? If so, question them by all means—ruthlessly and aggressively. What are the secrets about yourself that you feel you must keep hidden? What are the things you feel a need to display? Who you do feel certain has betrayed or wronged you? To whom are you convinced you have done irreparable wrong? Those lights illuminating your past may be so bright that they actually prevent you from seeing everything that's there. If you turn those bright lights off for a moment, do you find yourself in darkness? Or do you discover a candle glowing?

3. Realize that difficulties are more apparent than real

We have defined sharing as fundamentally counter to our nature as human beings. For this reason, we experience sharing as difficult, as if we were overcoming an obstacle in order to achieve a desired result. What we must understand, however, is that this difficulty is a function of our residing in the physical world, which Kabbalah teaches is not our true "home" at the level of our souls. In the physical world, sharing is like trying to put together a jigsaw puzzle in which the pieces don't quite fit. A certain amount of force is required, and we must learn to accept this. This is the best we can achieve in the world as it is. At the same time, we should realize that there is another dimension in which everything fits perfectly and no force is required. Moreover, that dimension is our real home. Our intentions and our actions in our present environment are really only means for connecting with that other level of being. The difficulty of sharing that we experience here really derives from the nature of the physical world—where the pieces don't quite fit—rather than from our own true essence.

This offers a new perspective on the spiritual work of sharing. The effort involved is really toward returning us to our true place of residence. Every positive action strengthens our connection to that source and thereby diminishes the difficulties we experience. Negative actions or intentions, on the other hand, distance us from home and multiply the obstacles in our path. When we embrace this idea, the spiritually healthy self-interest in sharing is clearly revealed.

At this moment in your life, is there a self-serving desire or a destructive action that seems tempting to you? With that desire or action clearly in mind, ask yourself if you really wish to make things easier for yourself, or make them more difficult. Do you want the puzzle to become harder to put together, or are you ready for it to become effortless? The answer may not be as simple as it seems. You may actually need to perform the negative action in order to learn where your real interests lie. So if you like, go ahead. If you do learn that lesson, whatever discomfort you experience will be well worth the price.

Practice charity

Charity is of course a subcategory of sharing, but Kabbalah gives it special attention. In fact, no area of life demonstrates the major kabbalistic teachings more clearly than the giving—and the receiving—of charity. The kabbalists tell us that true charity is not the compartmentalized experience that it often becomes in contemporary society. Charitable giving—*tzedaka* in Hebrew —isn't something we do once a year in order to earn a tax deduction. It's a fundamental part of our daily lives. It's a tool that's absolutely essential to the transformation of the giver. The fact that it materially benefits the recipient is also obviously worthwhile, but Kabbalah's focus is more on the spiritual effects than on the tangible results.

The power of charity springs directly from the one overriding characteristic of our existence in the physical world—that is, the ever-present power and temptation of the desire to receive for the self alone. Because this desire is encoded in our nature as human beings, our task is to recognize and resist it every day and every minute. Charity is an essential tool for exercising that resistance, for expressing it as proactive behavior, and for gaining the connection to the Light that proactive behavior always makes possible.

Kabbalah's perspective on the spiritual meaning of charity is rich and complex. It emphasizes that even for the giver, charity is as much about getting as it is about giving.

As always in Kabbalah, correct action has spiritual self-interest at its core.

When we give our money or our time or even our emotional support, we draw closer to the Creator. When we share what we have with others, we move toward oneness with God—and this is an extremely good bargain.

But if giving charity is an act of great merit, what about receiving? As you may recall from our discussion of the Light and the Vessel, Kabbalah teaches that unearned gifts are of little benefit to those who receive them, at least in a spiritual sense. Indeed, receiving charity is not in itself a positive action, but it can become one, depending on the awareness and the intentions of the recipient.

We should receive charity with the consciousness that we are bringing Light to the person who gives to us, and thereby to the world. We are providing an opportunity for that person to perform a righteous action, and Kabbalah teaches that providing such an opportunity is itself an act of merit. To our eyes, this may seem an unusual way of looking at charity, and possibly something of a convoluted one. The kabbalists explain it with an analogy. When there are no guests at an inn, the innkeeper has nothing to do. He cannot express his desire to be a good host or his talent for doing so. But when a guest finally arrives, the innkeeper is able to fulfill his nature. Far from feeling burdened by the guest, the innkeeper is grateful for the opportunity that has been provided. When the guest departs, the innkeeper can truthfully say, "Whatever I have done for you, you have done more for me." With an awareness of this paradigm, receiving charity can be understood as a righteous action equal to that of giving it. As the wheel of fortune turns, there may be times when we need the help of others. There is no dishonor in this. Indeed, it is an occasion for revealing Light through those who come to our aid, and Kabbalah urges us to understand it in that way.

Below are some suggestions for bringing the powerful spiritual tool of charity into your life. Although many of them involve money as the medium of giving, this can be understood symbolically as well as literally. In any of the exercises, you can replace "money " with "love," or "encouragement," or "words of kindness," if you prefer. But be sure you're not doing this just because it seems easier! Look into your heart to discover the form of charity that you really find the most challenging. You can be sure it's also the most cleansing, transforming, and revealing of the Light.

CHARITY IN ACTION

1. Give every day

Charity should play a part in your life every day. More specifically, whenever you are about to undertake something significant in any area—whether it's a business transaction, a change in a personal relationship, or moving to a new area of the country—recognize the importance of the moment by a charitable contribution. You should also say a brief prayer to connect the act with the Light. Express your intention to give and share in God's name. Tell the Creator that you wish to share the Light that He has revealed in you, and thereby to reveal even greater Light in the world as a whole.

2. Know what to give

The value of what you give is determined in your own heart, not by the IRS. At the same time, your charitable contributions should be significant enough to focus your attention. One Kabbalah student has evolved a good procedure for determining the amount of money he sets aside for charity over the course of a twelve-month period. Soon after the beginning of the year, he takes a quick look at his finances, decides how much he could comfortably give—and then doubles the figure. Are you ready to make a similar commitment? Perhaps not, if your present finances really won't allow it. But for many of us, the amount we give really depends on how sincerely we want to prepare ourselves as Vessels to receive the Light.

Quite understandably, people sometimes feel that their own finances are stretched too thin for them to give money to others. Kabbalah counsels against this. In fact, the benefits of giving are perhaps even greater when we have little: Sharing is an opportunity to experience a consciousness of wealth and magnanimity, rather than poverty and scarcity. And once again, the amount you give is insignificant compared to the meaning you attach to it. In this sense, less is often more.

An anecdote concerning a professional gambler may seem an unlikely reference point in a book about Kabbalah, but it exemplifies this principle very well. After winning a high-stakes poker tournament in Las Vegas, the gambler was interviewed by a national newsmagazine. The reporter mentioned that at one point the gambler had bet almost a million dollars on a single hand. Wasn't it difficult to risk that amount of money? The gambler shook his head and laughed. "Betting a million dollars is easy," he said. "What's hard is betting a nickel, if it's the last one you've got."

In the same way, a billionaire who endows a hospital or a library may know less about the real experience of giving than a person who really sacrifices in order to share. In the end, whatever amount you give to charity is the right amount—as long as it hurts just a little!

3. Start small

In order to make charity an ongoing part of your life, it's best to start small. Giving should become a habit or even a reflex, rather than a special occasion or an extraordinary departure from your normal routine.

A businessman in Chicago was having a difficult time accepting the importance of charitable giving. He was deeply moved by Kabbalah and had seen many positive changes in his life since he began studying, but money was where he drew the line. He worked hard to earn it, and he found giving money away to be almost impossible, even in small amounts. In a sense, this was a positive thing: since he felt great resistance to parting with even nickels, dimes, and quarters, it was possible for him to make great progress simply by altering this relatively minor behavior. It wasn't as if he had to do anything momentous, or anything that would really jeopardize him physically, emotionally, or financially. It was only a matter of confronting a strong, irrational inhibition.

Just before Shabbat, the businessman and his Kabbalah teacher discussed all this, and the teacher made a specific suggestion. For one week, whenever the businessman received any change for payment of any kind, he was to put the money aside for a charitable donation at the end of the week. It turned out to be a relatively small amount of money—less than twenty dollars in all—but saving this small change represented a big change in the businessman's consciousness. Several times a day it focused his attention on issues of charity and giving, and it caused him to confront his resistance to those righteous actions. At the end of the week, on Friday afternoon, he counted the money and made a charitable contribution of one kind or another in that amount. Usually he wrote out a check and mailed it to a deserving organization. Sometimes he left ten- or twenty-dollar tips for the hard-working waiters at the restaurant where he often ate lunch. Occasionally he gave away the change itself, though this often proved cumbersome.

In any case, he was amazed by the sense of fulfillment he derived from this activity. He found himself looking forward to each Friday, when, just before Shabbat, he decided where to send his weekly contribution. It seemed completely illogical and at odds with his hard-headed approach to finances, but he actually felt richer after he gave money away. As time passed and he began to give larger amounts, he felt richer still.

As you build charity into the foundation of your life, you may also want to start small. That's perfectly reasonable and commendable. The main thing is to develop an awareness of giving, and to be continuously in touch with this awareness.

4. Keep it quiet

We have mentioned the kabbalistic principle that what is concealed is always more powerful than what is manifest. This most definitely applies to charity. Kabbalah teaches that the highest form of charity occurs when the identities of the giver and the recipient are not known to each other. Of course, this is not always possible, and many people see no harm in knowing where their giving actually goes. But the principle of extreme discretion with regard to charity is essential, whether it involves support for a single individual or an organization.

Never expect reward or recognition for giving charity. If you really feel the need to get recognition for your support, you can take some satisfaction in knowing that your righteous action will eventually be known no matter how well it's been hidden.

And the longer it takes for the truth to come out, the more it will be appreciated. This may not be a spiritual law but it is an infallible one.

A Kabbalah student once told me how he'd gone to his employer to discuss an acute financial problem. The student's wife had needed emergency surgery during childbirth, but the company health insurance provider refused to cover the ten-thousand-dollar bill. The employer agreed to speak with the insurance company and advocate on the student's behalf—and a week later he informed the student that the insurer had agreed to cover the bill. It was not until several years later—after the employer's death, in fact—that the student learned that he had personally paid the ten thousand dollars. This is an example of true charity in its purest form. It also exemplifies the lasting power of charity. Today, whenever they look at their healthy young daughter, the Kabbalah student and his wife remember the man who paid the cost of bringing her into the world—and the concealed manner in which he did so only makes their affection for him greater.

5. Remember that money isn't everything

The biblical Book of Genesis presents Abraham the Patriarch as the very essence of sharing and generosity. The eighteenth chapter of Genesis describes his overwhelming generosity to three travelers (they're actually angels) who unexpectedly appear before his tent. Although Abraham was one hundred years old and had undergone circumcision only a few days earlier, he literally runs to be of service to the strangers. Although no money changes hands, this must certainly qualify as giving behavior, if not actually charity in the narrow sense. In order to be genuinely charitable human beings, we must be eager to open not only our wallets, but also our hearts and even our homes to other people. Often someone may need a kind word or something to eat much more than a cash donation. Moreover, it's often more difficult to really interact with a needy person than to simply give money—which is all the more reason to initiate personal contact.

In the legends of Kabbalah, the biblical prophet Elijah often appears disguised as a beggar or a homeless wanderer, and those who offer him hospitality are richly rewarded. You may or may not choose to believe that someone who needs your help is Elijah, but you can and should regard such a person as an opportunity to gain fulfillment and connection with the Light.

The great kabbalists of Safed made it a practice to see the innocent and beautiful child hidden within every person, regardless of the condition to which they might have fallen— and a child needs love and kindness and encouragement much more than money.

In offering charity, remember this precept and put it into action.

Pray

In the biblical Book of Genesis, Adam and Eve were expelled from the Garden of Eden for eating from the forbidden Tree of Knowledge. For his role in bringing this about, the serpent was also punished. The serpent was condemned to travel forever on his belly and, as the Bible puts it, *to eat dust all his life.* A great sage of Kabbalah, the Rabbi of Kotzk, was puzzled by this. What is the real meaning of this punishment? Is it not in one sense a blessing? Dust, after all, is everywhere. The serpent will never lack for food, which is more than many of the world's people can say. And what else does a serpent need besides food? How, the rabbi wondered, did the serpent get off so easy?

After some deliberation, the rabbi understood that since it lacked nothing, the snake's real punishment was that it would have no reason, ever, to ask the Creator for anything. By giving the snake all that it would ever need, the Creator indicated an intention to never hear from the snake again. This was the snake's punishment: It was cut off from God's desire that we draw near.

The Creator, on the other hand, *wants* to hear from us. The Creator is like a loving parent with grown children. Nothing makes parents happier than the knowledge that their children still need their company, their example, and their guidance. The explicit reason for a visit to our parents is much less meaningful to them than our desire for closeness itself.

In the same way, our presence brings the Creator great joy, and it is through prayer that this presence comes about.

Among new students, prayer is one of the most compelling aspects of Kabbalah. They *want* to pray, but they're deeply uncertain what prayer really is. In order to deal with this uncertainty, several common misconceptions about prayer need to be addressed. Many people intuitively think of prayer as a kind of dealmaking. Prayer is understood as a form of negotiation, and the terms are sometimes very explicit. We've all heard stories of people in crisis who sought to bargain with God: *"Dear Lord, deliver me from this avalanche and I'll worship you every day!" "Dear Lord, get me off this desert island and I'll build a hospital!"*

A corollary to this form of prayer is the idea that God ought to be praised and flattered as a way of laying the groundwork for our requests. A vignette in the Talmud describes a man who stood before the Holy Ark loudly declaiming his prayers. With a long list of adjectives, he heaped praise upon the Creator: "Thou art mighty, majestic, all-knowing, fearless, and without peer." The Talmud compares this sort of prayer with offering silver coins to someone who already owns a tremendous stock of gold. What does the Creator need with our prayers? Flattery may be an effective tactic in some areas of life, but it's irrelevant to the meaning and purpose of prayer.

But in truth, prayer is not simply a means to an end, not just a technique for telling the Creator what we want in an especially convincing way. It is not even a way of informing God of what we need; in any case, He already knows what we need. We must realize that prayer is an immensely worthwhile end in itself: a spiritual tool for opening channels of Light, a vehicle that carries us to God. Our prayers bring joy to the Creator even as they bring comfort to us. Prayer purifies, elevates, and transforms us. It awakens our souls.

Kabbalah describes two essential principles that we must grasp in order to fully experience prayer. First, we must recognize the *inner significance* of the act. We must realize that prayer is not about achieving a certain outcome in the material world, whether it's a new car or a cure for a serious illness. Prayer is not about creating a change in our bank accounts, our love lives, or our physical health. Instead, it's about changing, transforming, the state of our souls.

Second, we must have certainty that our prayers will achieve this supremely valuable spiritual goal. In other words, we must first understand the power of prayer, and then we must deeply trust in that power. Doubt is the great enemy of prayer. Even when we realize that the true purpose of prayer is inner transformation rather than success or acquisition in the external world, we may still doubt that transformation is possible for us. We may see ourselves as beyond hope, beyond redemption, and altogether "too far gone."

This, Kabbalah teaches, represents an insidious kind of self-devaluation that is really a form of arrogance. By describing ourselves as beyond the reach of the Creator, we assert that we are stronger than God. We are a problem that He can't solve. We are a lock that He can't open. There is no more pure expression of the negative side of our nature than this. By learning to banish doubt from our prayers, we can take a huge step forward in our spiritual journey.

The eighteenth-century kabbalist Rabbi Moshe Chaim Luzzatto wrote with great insight about prayer and its place in our lives. Rabbi Luzatto described the very possibility of prayer as an act of love on the part of the Creator. By endowing us with the power of prayer, God gives us the opportunity to experience His presence in the most intimate way—to discover His presence not somewhere up in the sky, but within ourselves. Nothing can compare with the beauty of that discovery. The joy of it is the true culmination of kabbalistic prayer.

Any exploration of Kabbalah and prayer must touch on the importance of the Hebrew language. As we've discussed earlier, it is a basic kabbalistic teaching that the letters of the Hebrew alphabet are more than the building blocks of a language—they are manifestations of the Light of the Creator. Kabbalah tells us that the Hebrew letters and the words built from them are like access codes granting us entry into the spiritual realm. In certain combinations, the Hebrew letters have the power to open us up to channels of Light in the Upper Worlds.

For this reason, a number of Hebrew prayers must be repeated not just every day, but several times throughout the day. This is not only for the meaning of the words, but also for the access codes encrypted within them. Beneath the surface of each prayer lies a system of hidden paths that lead directly to the emanations of the Light.

This is why kabbalists pray in Hebrew, and use the prescribed prayers. This is why Kabbalah urges us to scan the Hebrew text, even if we can't actually read it. The surface meaning of a passage is expressed in translation, but the spiritual power derives from the combination of Hebrew letters on the page.

Consider the following story.

An Open Heart

It was the New Year, and the Baal Shem Tov was having difficulty praying. His students were very concerned. They had never seen him have as much difficulty as he was having on this day. They knew, as did everybody else, that the Baal Shem Tov knew everything there was to know about praying. His prayers were said to plumb all seventy levels of supplication. Just being in the same room with him opened channels of Light unknown to other men. Still, with all he knew, he was having difficulty, and the students were worried.

Meanwhile, at the very back of the crowded synagogue, a little boy of five stood with his father. The boy's father, like the Baal Shem Tov, was concentrating on his prayers with all his might. The little boy looked around, as little boys will, and sure enough, everyone was concentrating just as hard as his father. Caught up in the spirit of the congregation, the boy yearned, more than anything else, to join in, to show his devotion. With this in mind, the boy opened the prayer book. He looked at the strange scribbles on the page and, of course, none of it made any sense. He closed the book. What could he do? He was at a loss. And now, wouldn't you know it, his nose was running. The boy reached into his pocket and pulled out a handkerchief. There, wrapped in the handkerchief, was a beautiful shiny whistle.

The boy wiped his nose and considered the whistle. His mother must have hidden it in his pocket for him to play with after the service. He thought to himself, "If I blow this whistle very hard, God will hear it, and He will know how much I want to be with Him." The little boy looked up at his father and pulled on his coat. "What is it?" his father said sternly. "I want to blow my whistle," the boy said. "You can blow it after the service," said his father and went back to his prayers.

"Hmmm," the boy thought. "After the service will be too late." So he pulled on his father's coat again. "What?" his father said, becoming annoyed. "I want to blow the whistle *now*," the boy whispered. His father narrowed his eyes, which was always a bad sign. "Don't you dare," his father mouthed, and he went back to his prayers.

It isn't clear what happened next. What exactly possessed the boy to disobey his father is a mystery. Perhaps the boy was simply stubborn. Or perhaps he was driven by something higher than his father. Whatever the case, the boy put the whistle to his mouth and, in a synagogue filled with only the quiet murmurs of five hundred devoted supplicants, he blew it as hard as he could.

The boy's father nearly jumped out of his skin. He could hardly believe what had happened. He reached down and snatched the whistle away from the boy. Everyone was looking at them. The boy's father didn't know what to do. He was not a man given to corporal punishment, but perhaps he had been too lenient with the boy. What difference would it make now anyway? The damage had been done. The father tried to stammer out an explanation to the congregation, but before he could get anything intelligent out of his mouth, he was interrupted by a well-known and kindly voice. "Did you blow that whistle?"

It was the Baal Shem Tov himself. "Well, actually," the father said meekly, considering the whistle in his hand, "it was my son. But he's only five and—" The Baal Shem Tov turned his attention to the boy. "Did you blow the whistle?" Bravely, the little boy nodded. "Why?" the Baal Shem Tov asked. "Because," the boy answered, "I can't read and I wanted to talk with God like everybody else." The boy's father started to apologize, but the Baal Shem Tov said, "I want you to know that your son's blowing of that whistle opened more gates to the Creator than I could with all my knowledge and prayers and meditations. Thank you."

This story reveals the pitfalls of concentrating on the technicalities of prayer—or of Kabbalah itself—to the exclusion of the true spiritual foundation. The power of prayer lies in our desire for closeness to the Creator, and the Creator's desire for closeness with us. Whether you pray in Hebrew or English—or even if you just look around at the world with the Creator in mind—there is no substitute for an open heart.

How to Pray

1. Love your neighbor

Rabbi Isaac Luria, the great sixteenth-century kabbalist, taught that we should precede every prayer with a sincere commitment to one of the most fundamental precepts of Kabbalah: "Love thy neighbor as thyself." This should not be done simply as rote behavior. We are not just reciting a formula. It should be a moment of focused attention in which we really commit ourselves to feeling love for other human beings, and to caring for their welfare with the same attention we give to our own.

When we make this commitment, the kabbalists explain, our prayers flow together with those of millions of other people, and thereby the power of our prayers is vastly multiplied. This is not just a metaphor. Kabbalah describes prayer in terms of manifest physical energy, like electricity or hydroelectric power. We can't see or hear the power of prayer, but it is by no means a mere abstraction, and its practical effects have been well documented.

2. Replace doubt with certainty

More than two hundred years ago, the great kabbalist Rabbi Elimelech made some observations about prayer that may strike a chord with many of us today. Rabbi Elimelech taught that whenever we pray, a negative angel appears beside us and whispers in our ear, "What's the use? Do you really think you can change yourself after all the terrible things you've done? You're beyond help, and praying can't possibly do you any good!"

If prayer is just beginning to become a significant part of your life, you may have heard that whispering. You have probably experienced some doubts. When you pray, there may be a part of you that's wondering, "Is this really going to work?"

It's best not to ignore those feelings, but neither should you trust them. Remember that the negative is always attracted to opportunities for positive transformation, just as surely as ants are drawn to a picnic. To deal with your uncertainties, be sure first of all that you're not falling into the trap of "dealmaking" with the Creator. If you're worried about whether your prayers will work, it may be that you're really worried about getting what you want. But this is not the purpose of our lives, and it is a misunderstanding of the meaning of prayer.

Our purpose is to become what we were meant to be—and the Creator is already giving us exactly what we need at this very moment to achieve that end. When you understand this, you'll see that prayers cannot work or not work in the sense that we can win the lottery or not win it. "Failure" can only occur if we don't create the heightened consciousness in ourselves that fosters connection with the Light. Bringing about this consciousness is in our own hands. It's not a matter of God hearing us and granting our wish.

Once you've understood that prayer is not about dealmaking, it's still essential to replace doubt with certainty. You can approach this very directly, perhaps in a new prayer that's explicitly concerned with your doubts. You should not pray while still harboring these fears and trying to ignore them. If you sense doubt in yourself, capture its energy by praying for doubt to be replaced by certainty. There is a Hebrew prayer explicitly devoted to this purpose, but you may prefer to simply put your own emotions into words. If you feel disconnected from the Creator and His Light, express those feelings. Don't ask God to make them disappear, however. Instead, speak of your desire to change and your intention to become a worthy Vessel for the Light. Accept responsibility. Then, when change comes, you can appreciate it in the full knowledge that you've earned it.

3. Pray the way that works best for you

Many prayers in Hebrew are designed to be spoken aloud. Just as the Hebrew letters have intrinsic spiritual power when they are printed on a page, the spoken words are similarly powerful. But prayers in English may be silent or spoken, and the choice is yours.

Rabbi Nachman of Bratzlav, a great sage of the eighteenth century and a descendant of the Baal Shem Tov, was known for turning his prayers into highly emotional "conversations with God." Speaking in the Yiddish vernacular, he cajoled, pleaded, and reasoned with the Creator, often shouting and crying—

anything in order to be made worthy and strong in his spirituality. Most often Rabbi Nachman would do this in private, sometimes sequestering himself in a garret or a storeroom, but his manner of prayer was certainly not kept secret from his students.

It may take many years before prayer becomes sufficiently ingrained to achieve this level of spontaneity, but it's something to aspire to. It represents a sense of intimacy with the Creator that's sadly remote from most people's experience. It also expresses a degree of extremely focused concentration that is fundamental not only to prayer, but to all the spiritual tools of Kabbalah.

The Hebrew word for this kind of concentration is *kavanah*. Most new students find that silent prayer is the best method for achieving this state. Over time, many begin to feel comfortable praying aloud. In any case, there's nothing to be self-conscious about. The Baal Shem Tov spoke about this very clearly. He said that if a drowning man thrashes about and flails his arms, we would never think to make fun of him. He's trying to save his life. In the same way, people who gesticulate in prayer are trying just as fiercely to keep themselves from being overwhelmed by the negative influences that are trying to distract them from connection with the Light. This is what prayer is really about. Pray in the manner that works best for you.

4. Pray for others

Prayer for others is one of the most powerful forms of sharing intention. As the kabbalist Rabbi Elimelech beautifully expressed it, this form of prayer represents a kind of spiritual embrace, or even a merging at the soul level. When we pray for another person, we interact with that person in a dimension that transcends the separateness of our physical bodies. We become one with the object of our prayers. We give our strength to another person and render that person as complete and healthy as ourselves.

As with other kinds of prayer, there is no need to beseech the Creator for specific physical outcomes or tangible results when praying on other people's behalf. Ask only that the Light may be revealed in them, that they become strong in following their spiritual path, and that the purpose of their lives might be fulfilled.

With these principles in mind, is there someone in your life at this moment whom you believe could be helped by your prayers? Without hesitation, say a prayer for that person right now. He or she will surely benefit. Just as surely, so will you.

5. Understand the answers

It sometimes happens that people are very frustrated by prayer. This is especially true when the purpose of their prayers is oriented toward a specific outcome. "I prayed that I would get into Harvard, but I only made the waiting list." "I prayed for a new car, and the next day my old one broke down." "My prayer for a raise got me fired." Beyond the fact that these prayers fall into the category of spiritual dealmaking, we must also recognize another very significant possibility: It's not that they were unanswered, but that the answer was no. When this is the case, we must realize that no is what's best for us, regardless of how unfair it may seem. Indeed, we should offer a prayer of thanks to the Creator for giving us exactly what we need or withholding what we don't need.

Another reason prayers sometimes seem to go unanswered pertains to our spiritual condition at the time of our praying. We live in a time when negative energies are very powerful. Since there is significant interference impeding our access to the Creator, we must make our prayers strong by doing our spiritual work beforehand. The situation can be compared to a radio station attempting to broadcast during a thunderstorm. If the signal is weak, the static electricity in the air can drown out the transmission, while a more powerful signal can still be heard clearly. When you pray, always ask yourself if you merit the response you wish, or indeed any response at all. As always, it's a matter of accepting responsibility.

In order to get what you want, be the person you ought to be. In fact, if you pray to be that person, getting what you want will take care of itself.

Practice Shabbat, the Sabbath

Before the world was created, God understood just how difficult the spiritual task of humanity was going be. The Creator knew that humanity was going to need all the help it could get. According to kabbalistic teaching, therefore, the Creator spoke with Moses in the primordial state. He told Moses that He had only one great jewel in His treasury, and He had chosen to give it to mankind. This was Shabbat, the Sabbath day.

Nothing in Kabbalah is more fundamental than the concept of Shabbat and its observance.

The Light we draw from any spiritual action depends on our understanding of that action's power. It's essential, therefore, to acknowledge, appreciate, and continuously explore the power of Shabbat throughout our lifetimes.

Our task in the world *is* difficult—and the closer we get to transformation, the harder our task becomes. Each day there are new trials and temptations. Our spiritual work, like our work in the physical realm, requires perseverance, diligence, and plain old-fashioned sweat. By the end of a week we may find ourselves worn down, worn out, and depleted. Knowing all this, the Creator gave us the Sabbath—one day just to sit back and cruise, if that's what we really want to do.

A new Kabbalah student once spoke with me about the tremendous appeal of the very idea of Shabbat. "Every day seems so full of responsibilities," he told me. "Both my wife and I have full-time jobs, because there are always bills to pay. But that's only the beginning. The car needs an oil change, the house needs to be painted, the kids need rides to a dozen different activities. What a relief it would be to have one day when everything is put on hold. A genuine day of rest." And it's true! Shabbat is a time when you can sleep all day or go to the beach. I believe, however, that doing so would represent a very large missed opportunity.

Suppose all the supermarkets got together and decided to do something to show appreciation for their customers. For one day, everything in the stores would be free. People could just load up their shopping carts and take whatever they want by the carload. Customers could make as many trips as they want. Come one, come all!

If something like this were to happen, there would undoubtedly be cars lined up for miles trying to reach the supermarkets. People would put everything aside to take advantage of this amazing opportunity. After all, everyone needs food, and it's just good sense to acquire it when it's free rather than when it's not. Still, not everyone would take advantage of the opportunity. In fact, despite the huge numbers of people who would converge on the markets, the chances are that a majority of people would not. They would go to a movie, or pass the time with friends, or perhaps just stay in bed. For most of these people, this would not even be a conscious decision. Mere inertia would prevent them from acting in their own best interests.

In exactly the same way, Shabbat is a day when sustenance for the spirit is available to us absolutely free, and with no strings attached. The only limit on the Light we gain during Shabbat is our capacity, as Vessels of the Light, to absorb it. By using the tools of Kabbalah to prepare the Vessel, we can maximize the opportunity. As always, there can be no coercion in spirituality. We have free will. We can choose passive over proactive behavior, despite the fact that each Shabbat is a God-given chance to achieve our genuine purpose in life, which is connection to the Light.

According to kabbalistic teaching, on Shabbat we revert to the spiritual condition of Adam in the Garden of Eden before the sin took place. Therefore, on Shabbat we do only spiritual work to draw and reveal the Light of the Creator, for on this day our desire to receive for ourselves alone does not block our connection to the Light. Indeed, this is the true greatness of Shabbat. Regardless of our immersion in self-serving desire, on Shabbat we are given the opportunity to be purified—not through any earned merit of our own, but simply as a gift from the Creator. We can ascend to a state in which we are totally pure and unhindered by the constraints of our physical existence.

Shabbat is filled with the pure unadulterated energy of the Light. It's a free glimpse into the future, when humanity will be transformed and every day will be filled with the fulfillment of oneness with the Creator. Shabbat is the only day on which we are not required to *earn* our transformation. In fact, the Light of Shabbat is so great that we couldn't possibly earn it. Again, only one thing is required of us: that we prepare ourselves as fitting Vessels in which the Light can come to rest.

Earlier we said the Light that we reveal depends upon understanding our power to reveal that Light. A related law pertains to the Sabbath:

The Light revealed on the Sabbath is equal to our understanding of how much Light is available to be revealed. And that amount of Light is literally without limit.

Shabbat, then, is most definitely a day on which we are free of the mundane responsibilities that fill our lives during the rest of the week. But it is not a day for doing nothing. On the contrary, Kabbalah presents us with a full range of activities and observances that begin on Friday afternoon and continue through Saturday evening. These are not only very powerful from a spiritual standpoint, but are also hugely enjoyable simply as human interactions.

In many families, for example, including my own, Shabbat is welcomed on Friday evening with an ancient song entitled *"Lecha Dodi."* Although at the time of this writing he's just two years old, my son, David, always knows when Shabbat is coming, and he loves to sing this song. It's difficult to describe the joy I feel at those moments, and I know the same joy is felt in countless other families. It's the happiness that comes from knowing what we came to this world to do, and knowing also that we're truly doing it. Our purpose is achieving oneness with the Creator, and on Shabbat there's an almost tangible sense that that purpose is being accomplished. And it's easy. In fact, it's a lot of fun.

Anything and everything of a spiritual nature is amplified on the Sabbath. Prayers have more influence. Meals have greater power to benefit body and soul. Study of spiritual texts is deeper and more revealing. All told, the Sabbath is truly a cause for celebration. It's like a magic token that's in our pocket throughout the week. Whenever we feel tired or dejected, that token gives us something to look forward to. The Sabbath is a positive guarantee of an opportunity on Saturday for rejuvenation and joy.

For me, an especially beautiful moment takes place each week just as Shabbat draws to a close. Late Saturday afternoon at the Kabbalah Centre, there's always a light meal followed by some singing of Hebrew songs. This has come to be known as "the third meal," to distinguish it from the Friday night Shabbat dinner and the early lunch on Saturday. The third meal is considered an especially rich spiritual moment; the belief is that it derives from a teaching of Rabbi Yehuda Ashlag. In the instant before the universe came into being, the thought of creation already existed in what we might call the mind of the Creator— and that thought contained the totality of all that was to follow. In the same way, the last moment of Shabbat encompasses every moment of the ensuing week. By filling that instant with joy, love, and oneness with God, we can make the next seven days equally full of Light. From beginning to end, Shabbat is truly a great gift.

OBSERVING SHABBAT

Kabbalah is the birthright of all humanity. It does not belong to any religion or ethnic group. It is the spiritual equivalent of fire, air, sunlight, or any other element of nature. These elements become available to us simply because we are human beings. True, we may choose to stay indoors throughout our lives, but at any time we can step outside and the world will be waiting for us. In the same way, you can begin to observe Shabbat right now, in the way that is most comfortable for you. As time passes, you may want to take part in more formal obser-vances—not because they are "right," but because they are more powerful tools for connecting with the Light of this sacred day. The choice is yours. The key is to recognize where you are right now on your spiritual journey, to acknowledge your desire to move forward, and to know that Kabbalah is always avail-able to help you in that process.

Here are some ideas for bringing the experience of Shabbat

into your life. No qualifications are needed. The only require-
ment is a sincere desire for connection to the Light of this special
day.

1. Wear something special

Since the time of Rabbi Isaac Luria and the other great masters
in Safed, Kabbalah has been linked to wearing white, and this is
especially true on Shabbat. More than the color, however, the
thought should be toward wearing something different from
what was worn during the rest of the week. Even if you wore
pure white clothing from Sunday through Friday, you should
wear *different* white clothes on Shabbat.

During the week, clean and set aside the things you intend
to wear on Saturday. This preparation is a way of bringing the
experience of Shabbat into the rest of the week. It calls attention
to the fact that a very different kind of day is coming even when
other days may seem more or less the same.

2. Be charitable

Friday night (*erev Shabbat* in Hebrew) is traditionally a time
for helping others. This should be done naturally, un-self-
consciously, and without ostentation. Charitable giving certainly
benefits the recipient, but Kabbalah teaches that generosity is
more than just altruism. Spiritually, the benefit is yours, through
preparing yourself as a Vessel to receive the Light.

3. Greet Shabbat

The arrival of Shabbat is inextricably a natural as well as a spiritual event. Greeting the Sabbath outdoors is a beautiful way of

recognizing this duality. In Safed, there were gatherings in the fields as the evening shadows descended on the mountains. Today, even in an urban environment, it's usually possible to welcome Shabbat for a few moments in the open air. In observant neighborhoods, there's a special feeling in city streets as Shabbat begins—many people believe the evening light is very different on Friday evenings. Finding out for yourself will bring a new dimension to your Shabbat celebration.

4. Sing Shabbat songs

The beautiful song *"Lecha Dodi"* is Shabbat's traditional musical welcome. But this is only the beginning. Songs are a wonderful part of the Sabbath dinner, and voices raised in Shabbat singing are said to bring great joy to the Creator. Dancing is also encouraged!

5. Give blessing

Shabbat is a time when the Light of the Creator is freely and openly accessible, and Kabbalah teaches that parents are the channels through which children receive the Light. It's the responsibility of parents to bless their sons and daughters, thereby connecting them with the Light to the greatest possible degree. A Shabbat blessing is given in a unique and very powerful way, with parents lovingly placing their hands on the heads of their children. This is a time to meditate on the wonder of physical touch as an expression of spiritual connection—and to remember that the Light we draw to ourselves and to our children depends on our understanding and appreciation of the

Creator's gift of Shabbat. The moment of blessing is a truly beautiful part of the Shabbat celebration.

The great kabbalist Rabbi Shimon bar Yochai is said to have taught the following parable: The Seventh Day appeared before the Creator and spoke in a sad voice: *The other days exist in pairs. Each has its soulmate, but I am alone.* And the Creator replied, *All of humanity will be your soulmate, and you will be the lifelong partner of every human being.* As in any deep and powerful relationship, our commitment to Shabbat requires understanding, attention, and a certain degree of sacrifice. And when we do our part, Shabbat rewards us a thousandfold. It has been said since ancient times that whoever truly keeps the Sabbath fulfills the entire Torah. From a kabbalistic perspective, there can be no more eloquent statement of the supreme importance and beauty of Shabbat.

Celebrate holidays and miracles

Passover, or *Pesach* in Hebrew, is one of the year's most beautiful and transforming holiday observances. A central portion of the observance is a large and long feast, during which the youngest member of the group is called upon to ask four traditional questions. The first of these questions—"Why is this night different from all other nights?"—could very well be asked about any holiday or ritual celebration. And for most people, the answer would seem obvious: "We celebrate holidays to commemorate some noteworthy incident in the past."

While this may be correct for relatively new, historically

based holidays such as the Fourth of July or Presidents' Day, it is most definitely not true of Kabbalah's deeply spiritual observances throughout the year. Although holidays such as Pesach do coincide with the calendar dates of ancient miracles, the purpose of these holidays is something much more pertinent to our lives than mere remembrance. Holidays are an opportunity not just to commemorate extraordinary events, but to connect with the spiritual energy that made them possible. A portion of the Pesach celebration, for example, pertains to the ten plagues that helped win freedom for the children of Israel from slavery in Egypt.

But Kabbalah teaches that Egypt should here be understood not just as the site of the pyramids; instead, "Egypt" is a code word for the slavery of self-serving desire and for the materialism that is an expression of that desire. We celebrate Pesach in order to connect with the Light that brought freedom from that bondage in the past and that can likewise bring us freedom right now. The ten plagues, moreover, are ten surges of Light that help destroy the darkness and negativity of the desire to receive for ourselves alone. When we recall the ten plagues at Pesach, we do so not as a historical exercise, but in order that we ourselves may be purified by this Light just as our forebears have been, not just in Egypt but wherever and whenever this holiday has been celebrated.

Holidays are specialized tools that we can use for connecting to particular forms of spiritual energy. Of course, we can also choose to ignore those tools, and many people do. Or if we don't entirely ignore the holidays that the Creator has given us, we may misunderstand them as simple commemorations.

Similarly, miracles can be understood as one-in-a-million occurrences that seem to override the laws of nature. But, like the conventional understanding of holidays, Kabbalah teaches that this is a fundamental misconception. Miracles sometimes do involve dramatic events that reveal the Creator's Light in the way that a bolt of lightning reveals electricity in the air. But miracles are really taking place all the time; if they seem rare, the reason lies within ourselves.

From a kabbalistic standpoint, a miracle is a manifestation of the Light in the physical world. Yet the Light is continuously manifesting itself, every second of every day, if only we had the consciousness to recognize it!

This teaching occurs many times in the kabbalistic texts, as well as in the Bible itself. In chapter 22 of the Book of Genesis, Abraham, his son Isaac, two servants, and a donkey travel to the foot of a remote mountain. There they gaze at the peak upon which one of the most dramatic incidents in the Bible is about to take place—the *akideh,* or binding of Isaac, in which Abraham shows his willingness to undertake even the most challenging of the Creator's tests. According to a *midrash,* or commentary on the Bible, Abraham and Isaac look up at the mountaintop, and Abraham asks his son what he sees. Isaac replies that there's a huge pillar of fire at the summit of the peak. But when Abraham asks the same question of the servants, they reply that there seems to be nothing unusual in view. Then Abraham tells the servants, "You don't see anything, and the donkey doesn't see anything either. So you stay here with the donkey." He and Isaac then ascend the mountain by themselves.

With respect to the miracles that take place at every moment, many of us are like the two servants—and the donkey! As it is said, *We have eyes, but we see not. We have ears, but we hear not.* Rav Berg often tells a story that makes this point very clearly. As a man was driving to work one morning, his car entered an intersection just as an oncoming vehicle failed to heed the red light. There was an accident. The man suffered a serious brain injury. An ambulance arrived promptly and rushed him to the hospital, but the only neurosurgeon who could save his life had gone off duty an hour earlier and had no doubt reached home by now. He could be reached by phone, but it would take at least three-quarters of an hour for him to get back to the hospital. This was more time than the injured man could wait.

But just then something completely unexpected happened. The neurosurgeon suddenly reappeared at the hospital. He had forgotten a gift for his wife that he'd intended to bring home, and he returned to the hospital to retrieve it. As a result, the injured man's life was saved.

Is this a miracle? Perhaps it is, of a very obvious kind. But remember that Kabbalah teaches that what is subtle and undisclosed is always more powerful than what is explicit and fully revealed. Suppose the man who was injured in the traffic accident had dropped his keys just as he was about to start his car. The time he took to find the keys was just enough time to cause him to miss the collision with the other car. If this seems a less miraculous circumstance than the neurosurgeon forgetting his present, it's only because it prevents the problem instead of solving it. Yet doesn't this make it a greater miracle rather than a lesser one?

Kabbalah tells us that these concealed miracles are taking

place all the time. We merit these divine gifts by becoming truly sharing beings and by performing acts of sharing in our daily lives. In our hearts and through our deeds, we connect with the Light and evoke the Creator's love in a million unseen ways. There is even a special prayer, the *mizmor l'todah* (prayer of thanks), through which we express thanks for the hidden miracles that are happening at every moment.

It may sound simplistic to say that every day is a holiday, and that every day is filled with miracles. But it also happens to be true, in the sense that the miraculous is really a function of the state of our souls, the accuracy of our awareness, and our choice to use the spiritual tools the Creator has provided for us.

Making Miracles Happen

1. Shift your perspective

Conventional thinking defines a miracle as an extraordinary happening, a sharp departure from the constraints of everyday reality. It's something startling, to be greeted with astonishment and wonder. But the outlandish aspect of miracles is really more a function of our expectations than of the happening itself.

Miracles happen when we not only begin to expect the miraculous, but when we begin to intend *it.*

To be sure, this is a counterintuitive way of thinking, at least at the outset. But it's also the means for transcending the limits that most people take for granted.

Questioning the obvious is a good way to start this process. Think, for example, of an object that you esteem rather highly. Without choosing anything that's very expensive or valuable to you, just identify something that you have every intention of keeping for yourself. Once you've thought of such an object, give it away.

If you're like most people, that last sentence gives you pause. You're not going to do it, are you? If that's the case, you've chosen to stay within the boundaries of everyday thinking and expectations—in which case you can't expect much more than everyday results, let alone miracles.

But suppose you really did give away something that you value? Although the object in question would then disappear, Kabbalah teaches that the emotion you invested in it would remain, though without its object of attachment on the physical level. This entity of pure feeling would become a magnet for the Light, which is always drawn to instances of true sharing. Now the equation that defines everyday reality has been altered. More Light makes more things possible. Enough Light makes anything possible. To the extent you choose, through positive action, to destabilize everyday reality, the Light will reward you with a new reality beyond anything you might have expected. But the first step is challenging your own instincts.

2. Pay attention to miracles

Over the course of a lifetime, most people develop very strong notions of the parameters of everyday reality. If you drop a shoe, it will hit the floor. If you lean against a wall, you won't pass though it to the other side. It's equally true, however, that most of us have experienced extraordinary departures from these constraints. Almost everyone has encountered remarkable synchronicities and incredibly fortuitous events. Yet the vast majority of people choose to classify these anomalies as insignificant and "just coincidence."

Why do we choose to devalue the miracles that have occurred in our lives instead of seeing them as glimpses into a higher reality? Is it easier to settle for the world as it is than to admit the possibility of the world as it might be? To explore your own feelings in this regard, make a list of some of the truly remarkable things that have happened in your life—for I have no doubt that such things have indeed taken place. Now, instead of relegating those events to the category of mere chance or meaningless coincidence, assume for a moment that there was a spiritual lesson in the occurrence. What could that lesson have been? Looking back, was there any need or intention on your part that might have brought that lesson into your life? And after the fact, was your behavior changed in any way—or should it have been changed?

3. Borrow on your *tzaddik*

It will certainly take many years, and it has probably already taken many lifetimes. But Kabbalah teaches that every human being will eventually achieve the spiritual perfection that is our true birthright. Eventually, each of us will achieve transformation and become the pure soul denoted by the Hebrew word *tzaddik*. And this is more than just a good person. A *tzaddik* is literally able to work miracles—and remember, at some moment in time you will be a *tzaddik* just as surely as at this moment you are reading these words.

In order to bring the power of miracles into your life right now, Kabbalah describes a very powerful tool known as "borrowing on your *tzaddik*." In a sense, this is a form of meditation in which we connect mentally, emotionally, and spiritually with the perfection that we will someday embody. We can draw on the spiritual power of this future self in order to bend the perceived laws of reality, in the same way that we might borrow money from a bank to buy a house. Borrowing on your *tzaddik* is a two-stage process. To begin, you must look at yourself in an entirely new way—not just as someone who *wants* to resist negativity or *intends* to restrict selfish desire or aspires to share with others, but as someone who has already attained that level of being. To the extent you can truly connect with this great soul—that is, your *tzaddik*—you will gain the power to create miracles. With all traces of negative energy erased from your being, a vast opening is created that the Light rushes to fill.

But this is only the first step. You must also take action in the real world. You must not only gain the power to work miracles, but you must also put that power to use with the same certainty that empowered the great kabbalists of the past, and even the matriarchs and patriarchs of the Bible. You must intend the miracle you choose, and then you must behave in accordance with the miracle you've chosen. You can—and you must—walk into the Red Sea. You can and you must make the sun stand still. This is the power of your *tzaddik*, but it is not fully realized until you actualize it.

Does this seem too much to expect of yourself? If so, please be aware that it is your doubt that creates the barrier, not anything in the external world. And be aware, too, that eventually your doubt will vanish and you will work miracles. It may be when you really have achieved transformation. Or perhaps it will be the next time you borrow on your *tzaddik*.

Study

In the town of Safed, I once visited the room in which the great Rabbi Isaac Luria studied the sacred writings more than four hundred years ago. It's a very spare, simple room but it's infused with the sense that miracles took place there—not miracles like the splitting of the Red Sea, but extraordinary achievements of the mind and heart. According to kabbalistic teachings, for example, Rabbi Luria's companion in study was the biblical prophet Elijah himself. Such was the intensity of Rabbi Luria's concentration that he was able to evoke the physical presence of the biblical patriarchs and matriarchs. When he read about Moses, Moses appeared.

While only great kabbalists are able to conjure the physical presence of biblical personages, this achievement differs in degree—but not in kind—from what always takes place when we study the sacred texts. Study is not a matter of intellectual *acquisition*, but an experience of spiritual *connection*. When we study mercy in the ancient texts, for example, we connect to the specific aspect of the Light that expresses mercy and brings it into our lives. Rabbi Yehuda Ashlag, who translated the Zohar into Hebrew, explained that this is the reason why study of the Zohar can be a more powerful tool for transformation than the reading of other texts. The Zohar is all about Light, while the Talmud deals with everything from the creation of the world to real estate transactions. A precept of modern cognitive psychotherapy is the idea that we become what we think about. Kabbalah would certainly agree.

When we study the Light, we become the Light.

The ideal conditions for study are quite clear in kabbalistic tradition. Though it may be impractical for people who work during the day, the best time for study is between midnight and dawn. There are several reasons for this. First, the discipline required to get out of bed and open a book develops commitment and focus. Indeed, Rabbi Ashlag wrote that the deepest benefits of his studies came from this discipline, rather than from anything he read or learned. Kabbalah also teaches that the hours before dawn are uniquely free from the negative energies that pervade the daylight hours like static on a radio. Studying late at night is a kind of kabbalistic stealth technology: It's an opportunity to sneak under the radar of the destructive forces.

For me, this experience began when I was about fourteen years old. My brother, Yehuda, and I read the Zohar, the works of Rabbi Ashlag, and the other sacred texts with our father, Rav Berg, as our guide. Kabbalistic teachings have been the focus of my life since childhood, but it was only when I started studying at night that I realized what studying Kabbalah really means. It's not about getting more and more wisdom, but about going deeper and deeper into the teachings over many years, and even over a lifetime.

How can I describe this experience of study, which took place not just once or twice, but night after night for many years? It was truly mystical, even magical. There really was a sense of being in the physical presence of the great teachers and patriarchs. The fact that this was a shared experience made it even more powerful. I trust that someday I'll be able to study in this way with my own young son—although for the time being I'm more interested in having him sleep through the night than waking him up to read the Torah!

I'm not aware that any other spiritual tradition explicitly values study to the extent this is true of Kabbalah. Without continual study, there is no hope for spiritual growth. This is a basic teaching of Kabbalah, and one that's often overlooked. Throughout this book we've emphasized the importance of awareness, understanding, and positive action in connecting to the Light of the Creator. But in the absence of study, these key elements of transformation are simply unattainable.

Why is such emphasis placed on study? Many fundamental ideas of Kabbalah are not particularly difficult to grasp. New students sometimes ask why they can't just start putting these ideas into action and leave further study to the scholars. After all, when we learn a new task—baking a cake, for example—we read the recipe, follow the steps, and thereafter we can bake cakes again and again without any difficulty.

But spirituality is different. Human nature dictates that even the most fundamental concepts, the simplest ideas, seem to disappear out of our heads. We can read a book about spiritual principles, and three days later we won't remember one word. Even worse, we lose sight of the practical application of what we learn. We face a spiritual dilemma, and suddenly nothing we've studied seems to apply. Kabbalah teaches us that this forgetfulness is not an accident, nor is it related to our intelligence or concentration. Rather, we forget spiritual teachings because our desire to receive for the self alone wants us to forget!

Forgetting our purpose, forgetting the spiritual laws, forgetting the kabbalistic tools of sharing—these are manifestations of the self-centered desire that is built into the human condition. Forgetting the fundamentals, in other words, is just an indication of our negative side doing its job. To combat the negative side, we must continuously make a conscious effort to remind ourselves of our purpose, and the best way to remind ourselves is through constant study. That's why it's so important to revisit Chapter 3, with its discussion of the Light and the Vessel and the nature of God and humanity.

The true subject of any spiritually oriented study is really the many manifestations of the Creator. Through study we come to know God and thereby to draw closer to Him, just as the patriarchs and matriarchs of the Bible came to know the Creator through personal interaction with Him.

Consider the life of Abraham the Patriarch. He was seventy-five years old when the Creator first spoke to him, and there were no spiritual writings to help Abraham deal with this extraordinary experience! In fact, the whole narrative of Abraham can be understood as the story of one man's on-the-job training in understanding and trusting the divine presence. It was an education that culminated in a very difficult final exam.

As recounted in the Bible, this took place when the Creator called upon Abraham to offer his son Isaac as a sacrifice. Secular writers have invoked the episode for vastly different and even contradictory purposes. Some have used it to condemn the brutality of Old Testament teachings—for who but a cruel and vindictive God would ask an old man to tie up his son and press a knife to his throat? But other authorities have seen the story as an allegory of the humane transition from human to animal sacrifice. Abraham, after all, does not actually go through with the killing of his son. In fact, strictly speaking, the Creator does not even demand that he do so. He only asks that Isaac be *offered* as a sacrifice, not actually made one.

And there are suggestions in the biblical text that Abraham might have known all along that he would not be required to sacrifice Isaac. For example, as they approach the heights of Moriah, which the Creator had specified, Abraham tells his servants, "You stay here with the donkey. The boy and I will go up there. We will worship and we will return to you." Why would Abraham speak this final sentence if he believed he was going to have to sacrifice Isaac? Several verses later, Isaac himself asks, "Where is the sheep for the burnt offering?"—and Abraham replies that "The Creator will provide the sheep." Is this wishful thinking? Or does Abraham know the Creator so well by this time that in his heart he's certain there will be a reprieve?

Kabbalah's teachings regarding this episode are very illuminating. Abraham is a person whose soul overflowed with the spiritual energy of mercy and kindness, which in Hebrew is called *chesed*. There are many instances in the Bible where this is made clear. Isaac, however, was an embodiment of *gevurah*, which is difficult to translate but includes the concepts of might and judgment. Kabbalah teaches that the true purpose of this episode was to temper the soul of Isaac with the energy of kindness—to literally bind this person who embodies the retributive aspect of justice, just as we must restrict this inclination in ourselves in all our dealings with the world. But perhaps there was a need also to temper Abraham's naturally gentle spirit with the reciprocal form of energy. In any case, the real meaning of the *akideh* has less to do with human sacrifice than with the completion of two great souls. Through them, the channels are opened for our own souls to become complete, for our own spiritual transformation to take place, and for our own oneness with the Creator to be achieved.

Amid all that was going on in this very complex story, the Scriptures make clear that Abraham completely trusted in the benevolence of the Creator. He betrays no hesitation at any point, for he knows that whatever happens will be for the best. After all, at this point in the biblical narrative he had been dealing one on one with the Creator for quite some time. Through some very trying situations, they had never let one another down, and Abraham had the opportunity to develop absolute trust in God through these personal interactions.

Abraham was a great patriarch. We may not merit the Creator speaking to us and listening to us in quite the same way that Abraham experienced. Nonetheless, through study of the biblical account of Abraham and the commentaries upon it, we can gain the same level of trust in the Creator that Abraham himself achieved. Just as a trip across the country can be made by plane, train, or automobile, we can arrive at the same destination as Abraham even though we rely on a different means of getting there.

In any human relationship, gradually accumulating knowledge about another person is both essential and very rewarding. This encompasses everything from facts about home towns and schools to thoughts about morals and ethics. Both literally and figuratively, it's a matter of getting to know who you are and where you're coming from. Our relationship with the Creator works in much the same way. Through daily study, we learn more about the Creator's nature, what motivates the Creator's presence in the world, and what the Creator expects of us. Although we can never understand the Creator the way we can another person, we can certainly know much more about His intentions for us in the world. Through this understanding, we strengthen our connection with the Light. We may not merit the Creator's speaking to us directly, but the more direct and intimate the relationship, the more promise the relationship holds. Bringing this about is the primary purpose of study.

A second way that study keeps us connected to the Light of the Creator is by putting us in contact with the *tzaddikim*, the righteous men and women who have come before us. They are people, generally from previous generations, who have shown through their work or through their writings that they are very highly developed spiritually. We can usually recognize *tzaddikim* in the same way we recognize great scientists—their thoughts and teachings are read and accepted by other *tzaddikim*, much in the same way that new theories in physics or mathematics are reviewed by peers.

By studying the writings of the *tzaddikim*, we avail ourselves of a higher point of view. The books of the *tzaddikim* are fundamentally different from everyday novels, biographies, or histories. The sacred texts of Kabbalah are gifts of the Creator that have been brought into the world by and through a small number of righteous human beings. Through their works, we are able to directly communicate with them beyond the limits of time and space, and across the borders between this world and the next.

It's as if our daily lives were lived in a maze bordered by high hedges. Kabbalah teaches that the *tzaddikim* are high above the maze telling us exactly which way to go at every turn, guiding us to our spiritual destination by the shortest possible route. And they do more than just give direction. Just as we can with the Light itself, we can create an intimate connection with the souls of righteous men and women who lived in the physical world and who remain available to us in the spiritual realm.

Even more than their teachings, this soul-to-soul contact with the righteous is vital to our spiritual progress. Our contact with these great souls magnifies our own souls' greatness. Because ego is so completely absent from their works, Kabbalah teaches that the writings of the *tzaddikim* have a quality of divine inspiration. Light flowed so directly to the *tzaddikim* that their writings are considered actual messages from the Creator.

Clearly, study goes beyond the exercise of our intellectual abilities. It's more than a supplement to our techniques of transformation. On the spiritual level of being, study is necessary for our growth and even our survival. It is truly food of the soul. Without continuous study of the sacred texts, the soul does not receive an absolutely essential element of its nourishment. And from a kabbalistic viewpoint, I want to emphasize that study of the Zohar is especially crucial.

Of all the sacred texts, the Zohar is the most effective instrument for connecting to the Light.

Without in any way diminishing the importance of the Torah or other divinely inspired works, the Zohar's power to cleanse and nurture the human soul is unique and incomparable.

I feel I should also address some of the questions and perhaps criticisms that have been brought up around this topic. How, for example, can the Zohar bring so many benefits when hardly anyone can understand it? After all, it's very difficult to make sense of the Zohar even in English, yet Kabbalah urges us to scan the pages in Hebrew!

In response to this, I must return to the metaphor of study as food for the soul. Very few of us understand the biology of digestion. Only a highly trained physician or scientist can describe the process whereby a piece of bread or a sip of orange juice is metabolized by the human body. Yet we are so constituted that we know, through the physical sensation of hunger, that we need to eat and drink. We may not understand all the hows and whys, but we are aware that this need must be satisfied, and we experience the consequences if it isn't.

Similarly, on the spiritual level, I promise you that our souls need nourishment just as much as our bodies. Problems arise, however, when the absence of physical sensations such as hunger or thirst lead us to ignore the very real possibility of spiritual starvation. We must feed our spiritual needs. The importance of doing so, and our ability to do so through texts like the Zohar, has no more to do with understanding than does our ability to digest a handful of peanuts.

Study in and of itself allows each of us to connect to the source and essence of the Creator Himself, and it facilitates the same connection for all humanity. The sages of Kabbalah taught that whoever studies the sacred writings brings peace. The Hebrew word for peace is *shalom,* and this word has a very intimate, personal connotation. It does not refer to world disarmament, or treaties between nations, or legislation to promote handgun control. For even if all these worthy large-scale goals were to be achieved, but discord remained between husbands and wives, brothers and sisters, parents and children, or even within the hearts of individual human beings, what would really have been achieved? Therefore, when the sages speak of peace through study, they refer to peace within ourselves.

When each of us is at peace with the person we see when we look in the mirror, strife between nations will cease. And all this begins with study.

STUDY IN ACTION

1. Know where you're starting from and where you want to go

Study should be done with a purpose, but not necessarily with a goal. We do not study in order to get something or even to learn something, but to be someone who is worthy of the sacred books that lie open before us and of the Light that's revealed by them. Bring this intention clearly into your mind before you begin to read. Take a moment and focus on the person you want to become through the experience of study: a sharing person, a person connected to the Light, a better person at the completion of your study than you were at its outset. You might even want to state this aspiration aloud: "Let my heart, mind, and soul be open to the Light."

2. Pay attention

Study requires focused awareness, and you should use all the practical tools available to cultivate this in yourself. Dress comfortably but respectfully when you read the sacred texts. Sit alertly, or better yet, stand up. Many of the great sages, it is said, stood for hours as they studied, often swaying slightly back and forth with rapt attention to the task. The Baal Shem Tov urged his students to study with deep fervor, using all their strength, until they literally broke out in a sweat.

3. Give thanks

A new student once told me about a certain biblical passage that had been puzzling her. It was the opening of the eighteenth chapter of the Book of Genesis, which reads, "The Creator appeared to Abraham in the oak groves of Mamre, as he sat at the entrance to his tent in the heat of the day. Abraham lifted up his eyes, and behold, three men stood near him." How could it be the Creator who was appearing, when the text says that Abraham looked up and saw three men? After thinking about this for some time, the student realized the need for a distinction between what appeared to Abraham inwardly—in his heart, when he was looking deep within himself—and what appeared physically before him when he "lifted up his eyes." The moment of this insight was a potent one for this new student of biblical texts; powerful not only intellectually, but as a genuine emotional and spiritual experience in its own right. The happiness she felt was beautiful to see, and I urged her to give thanks for this wonderful gift that she had received.

Remember: the deepest purpose of study is not just to gain knowledge or erudition or to stockpile intellectual ammunition for learned conversations. The real purpose is to discover the Light in ourselves through the medium of the sacred texts. When that discovery takes place and when we experience the happiness that it brings, we should joyfully give thanks to the Creator.

4. Scan the Zohar

The Zohar, like the Torah and other sacred writings, is more than a book in the ordinary sense of the word. The Zohar is a spiritual resource through which we can connect with the Light—and the Light, of course, manifests itself in an infinite variety of forms. Certainly the insights and intellectual revelations that come to us through the Zohar are expressions of the Light, but they are by no means the only ones, and perhaps not even the most valuable. Kabbalah teaches that simply by *looking* at the Hebrew letters that comprise the pages of the Zohar, we achieve connection with the Light of the Creator, regardless of whether we are able to read Hebrew.

This practice of "scanning" the Zohar has mystified newcomers to Kabbalah, whose notion of a book's importance may be limited to its intellectual content. The power of the Zohar, however, lies not only in what it means, but in what it *is*. The Zohar is a spiritually charged object. Just as we can receive an electric shock from a powerful battery even if we don't understand how it works, we gain benefit from scanning the pages of the Zohar even if we don't "understand" a single word of the text.

To some extent, it's difficult to place scanning in a particular category of spiritual tool. I've identified it with Study somewhat arbitrarily, primarily because it involves books. Scanning might also be called a form of meditation, but it doesn't really depend on focused contemplation of the letters or introspections derived from them. It's simply a matter of exposure. And if this sounds far-fetched, remember that many great things in life are meant to be experienced rather than explained.

If you have access to an edition of the Zohar in Hebrew, open it at random to let the power and beauty of the Hebrew letters enter your consciousness. This is especially beneficial during times of physical or emotional distress—when you're ill, for example, or worried about some pressing issue. Scanning is a technique that has been part of Kabbalah for thousands of years. To discover why this mystical practice has so long endured, try it yourself!

Practice introspection and meditation

Spirituality can become routine, and it can also become overshadowed by the seemingly more pressing concerns of our daily experience. Most people begin their spiritual work with a certain excitement. Perhaps they've reached a point in their lives at which they've begun to question the goals and motivations that had once seemed so convincing. They may be a bit confused, or even depressed, and suddenly they realize that there's a whole other way of looking at things. They're excited by spirituality in general and Kabbalah in particular. They consider the available spiritual tools and choose what seem the best ways to gain connection with the Light. And then they get started. Oddly, however, what at first seemed so exciting gradually becomes a new kind of routine. They settle in. A kind of rote spiritual practice gets going. It may be quite satisfying, but it's no longer really challenging. Observing the rituals and saying the prescribed prayers becomes comfortable. And without real awareness of what's happened, the true purpose is obscured.

Genuinely spiritual people experience every moment to the fullest. They are determined not to become blind to the reality of our place in creation and our purpose in life. They use all the tools available to maintain that awareness every minute of every day, or as close to that ideal as possible. Religion, on the other hand, often denotes a compartmentalized experience of orthodoxy for one hour or one day and obliviousness the next.

In this sense, I want to make it very clear that Kabbalah is not about religion as usual. It's not about rote behavior. It's not about doing things just because someone—even the Creator—wants you to do them. I've referred to many of the topics in this book as tools in order to emphasize their practical importance and to distinguish them from conventional religious observances. The tools of Kabbalah were given to us for very specific ends: to allow us to care more for others, and thereby achieve transformation.

Spirituality is fundamentally an internally motivated experience, and it is its own reward. This is made very clear by a passage in the First Psalm: *". . . the teaching of the Creator is his delight, and he studies that teaching day and night."* Notice that spiritual practice is called *delight*, not *obligation* or *daily routine* or *habitual behavior*. To me, the meaning of the verse is this: A truly spiritual person joyfully expresses and experiences spirituality in everything he or she does. This is what living according to the teachings of Kabbalah really means.

The Near-Catastrophe and Its Lesson

Several years ago I was driving down a busy street in Queens, New York. To this day I don't know exactly what happened, but without warning I lost control of the car. It was veering off to the left, then lurching over the low concrete divider that separated the traffic lanes. I had often heard that time seems to slow down at such moments, but I had never really understood what that meant. Now I seemed to be living in a dream, with a kind of leisurely sense of unreality that stretched out the moment like a rubber band. Then, suddenly, it was over. I was back in the world. Specifically, I was in the left-hand lane on the other side of the street, facing in the opposite direction from the way I'd been traveling. The engine was still running, but the car had stopped. Looking up, I saw a gas station nearby and pulled into it. An attendant checked the car and found nothing wrong, and in a few minutes I was back on the road.

For the next few minutes I was more frightened than I had ever been in my life—but only for a few minutes. Soon things started getting back to normal. Nothing had really changed. My attention was no longer on survival, but on getting where I wanted to go on time.

I often think of that nearly catastrophic incident on the street in Queens, and I've learned to deeply value its memory. I've come to depend upon it as a reminder of how precious every moment really is—or could be—if we could resist the temptation to just let the routine take over. I've learned to use this memory as a measure of what my spiritual awareness is compared to what I would like it to be. It's become a tool for introspection.

For this reason, Kabbalah discusses introspection as a way of keeping track of spiritual progress. Introspection isn't a matter of asking yourself if you've been studying the right books or praying for the right amount of time. It means asking yourself, "Is what I'm doing bringing me closer to the transformation of my nature?" Or, even more simply, "Do I care more for others than ever before?" or "Am I sharing more with others than I have in the past?"

If you ask these questions sincerely and with an open heart, you will receive a true answer from the depths of your soul. But be prepared. At a moment of real introspection, everything is up for grabs. You may need to completely change course. But without this critical analysis, we are limited to an empty spirituality that follows the letter of the law but not the spirit.

Since the time of the great kabbalists in Safed, meditation has been a highly developed tool for looking into our hearts, for fostering positive change both spiritually and in the conduct of our everyday lives, and for bringing the Light of the Creator into our hearts, our minds, and even the physical locations we occupy. For many people, meditation is probably understood as a relaxation method—and this may be an accurate description of some forms of meditation.

But Kabbalah views meditation much more proactively. Meditation takes us deep inside ourselves for an encounter with the true purpose of our lives, and what we must do to accomplish that purpose both now and in the years to come. Kabbalistic meditation does not transport us to some tranquil cloud far removed from the world's challenges. Instead, meditation shows us the reality of those challenges, stripping them of the negativity that so often attaches to them. It's a cliché to assert that problems are really opportunities, but it's also a great truth. Bringing that truth clearly into our awareness is one of the most valuable benefits of the meditation experience.

Kabbalah includes many methods and varieties of meditation, all of which share a number of well-defined steps that precede the actual experience of meditation.

The first step is an unflinching self-assessment. Before we can understand any of the complex issues that meditation can help to clarify, we must make a sincere effort to understand ourselves. And Kabbalah tells us that true self-understanding inevitably leads to a very specific conclusion.

We realize that we must take full responsibility both for who we are as human beings and where we are on life's pathway.

We did not appear in this world by chance. According to kabbalistic teaching, we chose our present incarnation as a vehicle for completing our *tikkun*—a word that can be variously translated as the *correction,* or *repair,* or *mending,* of the soul that needs to be completed in order for our transformation to be attained.

What an astonishing idea this is! It means that you alone are the cause of who you are. You, the person reading these words, did not come about through a process of random selection at the cellular level; rather, it was a process of conscious decision that took place on a spiritual plane. And by extension of this decision, whatever is present or missing from your life right now is your responsibility. The first principle of kabbalistic meditation is to fully embrace this idea. It allows us to move beyond any need to blame others for what we lack or to feel in debt for what we have achieved. Once we've reached that point of clarity, we can focus on the things we want and need to change.

While the first stage of kabbalistic meditation is a process of self-recognition, the second is one of *connection.* We must make a conscious, focused decision to connect with the Creator's Light, fully aware that the Light is always there for us whenever we sincerely desire it. There is a long tradition of kabbalistic meditation practices for making this connection, many dating from the time of Rabbi Isaac Luria in the sixteenth century. Some of these techniques are very demanding spiritually, and even physically. They demand great concentration and can take years to master. But other methods, such as those described below, can be quickly learned and put into practice. And there is immense benefit to doing so. Rabbi Luria himself is said to have stated that meditation for the purpose of achieving oneness with the Creator is many times more valuable than even Torah study.

More specifically, meditation reveals that connection with the Light can be an inwardly directed process. The divine presence is both within and without, and our task is simply to discover and reveal it in all things. In study and in prayer, our attention is directed toward sacred texts or spiritual realms that are outside our own being. In meditation, we look into our own hearts. It's a matter of opening ourselves rather than entering or ascending to an external spiritual realm or level of consciousness.

KABBALISTIC MEDITATION TECHNIQUES

1. Practice breathing meditation

Chapter 2 of the Book of Genesis reads, "The Creator formed man of the dust of the ground, and breathed the breath of life into his nostrils." As always in Kabbalah, this passage is interpreted as something that happened at a particular moment in time, and also as a process that is continuing even at this moment. Breathing meditation is first of all an awareness of that ongoing process. With every breath we take, we once again receive life from the only giver of life. But that, of course, is only half the story. With every exhalation we return something of ourselves to the universe. We quite literally share the atoms and molecules of our physical selves with other living things, thereby perpetuating life itself. It's difficult to think of a more routine and mundane task than breathing, but there's no human action that more closely replicates the Creator's giving life to humanity.

To practice breathing meditation, you'll need a quiet space and a few minutes of uninterrupted time. Begin by sitting comfortably but alertly in a chair, or cross-legged on the floor if you prefer. Close your eyes and breathe normally, but focus your attention on the process that's taking place. Feel your chest expand slightly when you inhale. Then, as you exhale, feel your lungs contract. After a few moments, turn your thoughts from the physical experience of breathing to the spiritual dimension that's so often overlooked. As you inhale, realize that the breath of life is entering you just as it entered Adam in the Garden of Eden—and realize also that this breath comes from the same source, which is the Creator. With this thought in mind, hold the breath for a few seconds and fully experience the sensation of the divine presence entering your being. Then release the breath and feel the opposite but equally powerful process that this represents: Just as the Creator has come to us and become one with us, we also reach out to the Creator. Our thoughts, prayers, fears, and hopes go straight from our hearts to God.

This mutual sharing, this circuitry that is the process of life itself, is made very clear and tangible through breathing meditation. As with so many spiritual principles, the pace of our lives may cause us to overlook the hidden wisdom of our breathing—but once we discover it, this wisdom is a constant reminder of our connection with the Creator and an instantly accessible conduit to the strength that connection brings.

Continue your breathing meditation for as long as you wish,

and then gently return your consciousness to the everyday world. As you open your eyes, you may feel as if you're somehow seeing everything for the first time. For a few seconds, you may literally feel reborn. This is a great gift, and one of the real benefits of breathing meditation. Let it inspire you to live each moment with renewed commitment to becoming a truly sharing person, and to nurturing that same transformation in everyone you meet.

2. Meditate on sacred verses

This method is especially beneficial for dealing with negative emotions such as fear, anger, or guilt. Any action we perform with a pure heart and with sincere desire for the Light immediately connects us with higher orders of wisdom and spiritual energy, and certain actions express our desire for the Light with particular clarity. Such an action could include opening the Bible—especially the Book of Psalms, or the Five Books of Moses, which make up the Torah.

To begin this meditation, open the Bible to a page at random and, without looking at the text, place your right index finger somewhere on a page. Then look at the verse on which your finger has come to rest and say it aloud.

As you do so, remember this kabbalistic teaching:

There are no accidents; everything happens for a reason, including the biblical verse you've just selected.

Although it may seem unrelated to your present situation, you should use this verse as a meditative tool. Think about it, and try to understand how it pertains to your current needs.

Repeat it subvocally again and again over the next twenty-four hours. In this way, you can replace negative thoughts with the word of God.

Many people have found this technique to be uncannily powerful. It's an excellent way to discover the power of the Light in a seemingly random occurrence. However, the use of sacred verses as objects for meditation does not have to be dictated strictly by chance. If you have a favorite biblical passage that moves and strengthens you, repeat it silently until it becomes an ingrained part of your consciousness. Or even say it aloud in situations that might otherwise be fraught with negativity, such as driving in heavy traffic or waiting for an important telephone call that's overdue.

Focus your consciousness not only on the meaning of the words, but also on the words as instruments for connecting with the Light of the Creator. Become aware of how your feelings change when you repeat the passage. Have the conscious intention of using the passage for inner transformation and enlightenment. And have trust in the Creator, who is literally the author of the words you have chosen.

3. Practice spiritual conversation

For new students, one of Kabbalah's most surprising teachings concerns the Creator's desire that we should draw close to Him. For some reason, perhaps resulting from shallow interpretations of the biblical narratives and their depiction of God, many people believe that God expects us to fend completely for ourselves—that the Creator "doesn't want to be bothered" with what's going on in our lives.

This negative belief is hugely destructive and represents a complete misinterpretation of the relationship between God and man. Like a loving parent, the Creator deeply desires our trust, our communication, and our closeness at every level of being. This meditation is designed to put you in touch with that experience of closeness.

As with breathing meditation, set aside some time in a quiet place where you will not be disturbed. If possible, this should be a darkened room illuminated by only a single candle. Sit comfortably but alertly in a chair or on the floor, and literally speak to God about the matters that are closest to your heart. If speaking aloud feels uncomfortable at first, it's all right to sub-vocally express your thoughts during your initial experiences with this exercise. But be aware that the difficulty of this meditation is an aspect of its power.

Where is your resistance really coming from? Primarily, it's the sense that you're sitting in a dark room talking to yourself. It's a lack of trust in the idea that you can really be in the presence of God. Struggle against this failure of trust, and realize that the struggle itself is inherent not only to this meditative experience, but to your true spiritual transformation. Struggle also to express yourself forcefully and even passionately, as you might speak to a close relative whose deepest desire is to help you, but who needs for you to make yourself known.

This should not be confused with asking for something. Remember: The Creator knows what you need, and in fact what you need is exactly what you're getting at this very moment. The purpose of this exercise is not to pass along information, but to foster the experience of intimacy with the Creator.

When you've finished speaking, sit quietly and pay close attention to the response your conversation has elicited—for there surely will be a response, if you've spoken sincerely and with complete honesty. You will gain insight into the deepest issues of your life. You will get a glimpse of the kind of connection that existed between the Creator and the great sages of Kabbalah, and you will want to make that connection the foundation of your life's every moment.

4. Practice listening meditation

This technique shares some elements with spiritual conversation, but its underlying principle is fundamentally different. Here, instead of expressing yourself fully and without inhibition, your efforts are turned toward completely silencing your inner voice in order to truly listen to the world around you.

"As above, so below" is a key principle of Kabbalah. Another way of expressing the same idea is that the microcosm contains the macrocosm.

Listening meditation allows you to experience this principle by focusing all your attention on the sounds of life all around you—and doing so with an awareness that every single one of them comes from the Creator. Rather than delving deeply into yourself, as in many other techniques, the purpose here is to *forget yourself* and thereby see the truth more clearly.

Unlike some other methods, you can practice listening meditation virtually anywhere. The technique depends on turning off your inner dialogue as completely as possible, and giving total attention to the sounds in the world around you. Depending on where you are, these may include birds singing or wind blowing through trees. More likely, you'll hear cars passing on the street outside your window or snatches of a television program from the apartment next door. Yet the Word of God is present—though perhaps well hidden—in all these sounds. You can hear the Word of God by, for a moment, removing the meanings you've attached to physical reality.

As you listen, your own thoughts will inevitably insert themselves between you and the world around you. When this begins to happen, stop for a moment, make a conscious effort to silence your inner voices, and then return your total attention to the external environment. Be aware that the benefits of this meditation lie in quieting your own thoughts as well as in tuning in to the world outside.

5. Practice creating love and forgiveness

Kabbalah teaches that our purpose in life is to transform ourselves into beings of sharing, to reveal the Light of the Creator, and to make our own nature one with God's. Toward this end, powerful tools have been provided for us in the physical realm—and meditation is one of the most powerful of all—but just as certainly, traps and pitfalls have been laid in our way. Simply put, the single most important step we can take toward achieving unity with the Creator is to love and forgive other human beings *unconditionally*, as the Creator loves and forgives us. It is also the most difficult step to take, with the temptations of anger, envy, and self-serving desire always seeking to divert us from the goal. Achieving our most worthy aspirations amid the negativity that surrounds us is what spiritual work is all about.

The meditation described at the end of this section is an excellent tool for making love and forgiveness integral to your dealings with other people, especially those toward whom you now harbor negative feelings. In order for the meditation to be effective, it's important to understand and accept three key principles:

1. Know that every human being who has come into your life, or who is part of your life now, or whoever will be part of your life, was sent by the Light to help you move forward along your spiritual path.

2. Know that any negative or destructive emotions you direct toward any of these people do not originate with them. They do not even originate with you! They are barriers placed in your way in order to prevent you from connecting with the Light.

3. Know that reaching higher levels of spiritual growth requires you to remove these barriers from your heart, using meditation and the other tools of Kabbalah. The alternative is many years of unnecessary frustration and pain.

Please take a moment to think about these principles, and how your life would change if you were to make them part of your daily experience in the world. Then, in a quiet place where you won't be disturbed, begin the meditation described below. You'll need a pen or pencil and a blank sheet of paper.

Begin by thinking about a relationship in your life that you would like to improve. It could be with someone you see every day, or it might be with a person you haven't seen in many years, but who remains a presence in your thoughts and emotions. Very often this is someone who is more important to you than he or she might realize. You may never have told this person about your feelings. You may have tried, but found that everyday channels of communication just didn't work. Write this person's name on a sheet of paper.

Now take a deep breath and feel the Creator's Light pouring into your presence. Feel it inside yourself, filling your body and soul, and feel it all around you, creating a luminous aura in which you're completely safe and protected.

Look at the name you wrote on the paper. See the name from your point of view, as a symbolic representation of another human being. Experience all the feelings you have for that person, even the negative ones. Be aware of how those feelings are kindled and attached to the letters on the page.

As you continue to look at the name, shift your point of view to that of the Light. From this higher perspective, the letters on the paper are just tracings of ink. In other words, there's nothing coming from the letters. So much is happening in your mind and heart as you look at those letters, but it's all happening within you.

Examine those thoughts and feelings with honesty and without fear. Fully experience the emotions that flood your consciousness. Realize that these sensations are not attached to the other person, and that they're certainly not built into the paper and the ink. They're *all yours,* and they're a barrier between you and the Light.

Now, mindfully, completely, and with full awareness, let go of those emotions so that you can embrace the Light. You may want to make a conscious decision to forgive the other person, but it's important to realize that the forgiveness is a completely internal process that really doesn't involve anyone but you. Forgiveness, therefore, really means releasing your spirit from the baggage and bondage that prevents it from transforming. When you make a genuine effort of this kind, Kabbalah teaches that angels will appear to guide and support you on your way to freedom.

Conclude by sitting quietly for a few moments, reflecting on the work you've just done. Then throw away the piece of paper. Crumple it up or tear it into tiny pieces. You may even want to burn it. Cast it out of your life in a way that shows how completely insignificant it is. The letters on that page mean nothing, and they never did. What matters—what always matters—were the feelings that filled your heart, and now your heart is filled with Light.

6. Practice music meditation

The sages tell us that music was not brought into the world just to entertain us. The purpose of music is to elevate our spiritual frequency, and it is a very effective medium for that purpose. In fact, it is easier to alter your consciousness with music than with any other spiritual tool.

Music was a very important part of spirituality in ancient times, especially before the destruction of the Temple in Jerusalem. It was also integral to the practice of Kabbalah in Safed and during the lives of Rabbi Isaac Luria, Rabbi Moses

Cordovero, and the other great teachers. There have also been times when efforts were made to suppress music as an element of spiritual work—to suggest that the joy engendered by beautiful music was somehow sinful or disrespectful—but this repression is only proof of music's transformative power.

Although specific songs and music selections are traditionally associated with certain special occasions, such as Shabbat or the various holidays, any singing or playing of a musical instrument is inherently powerful and positive. As a meditative tool, many people find that it's best to sing or play alone—not only for the sake of one's listeners, but in order to shed the inhibitions that often burden amateur musicians. Just let it rip, and realize that however you might sound to the music critics, your music is a joy to the Creator as long as it lightens your heart and brings happiness into your soul. Group singing is also a positive and transforming experience, especially with members of your family.

One caveat: The experience of making music is qualitatively different from only listening to it, especially if the source is an electronic device such as a CD player or a radio. Hearing music in this way can be healing and uplifting, but it's not what the kabbalists had in mind when they spoke of music as a tool for transformation. "Make a joyful noise unto the Creator" is how the psalmist put it—so go for it.

7. Practice proactive visualizations

These meditations are in some respects more specifically focused and goal-directed than the others we've discussed. They're strongly oriented toward action in the external world, rather than toward internal, subjective experiences or insights. Although they make use of contemporary settings and technologies, they are based on traditional kabbalistic ideas and techniques. Indeed, many ancient stories of the great sages of Kabbalah can be understood as carefully guided visualizations.

The Movie Screen

Once again, begin in a quiet space where you can be sure of some uninterrupted time. The first meditation includes two distinct steps, both of which involve visualization. Visualization is itself a powerful meditative technique about which many books have been written, but for our purposes here it's quite easy to put into practice.

Sit comfortably in a chair or on the floor, and close your eyes. Very gently roll your eyes upward as if you were looking at the ceiling, hold that position for a moment, then bring your eyes back to a relaxed position while still keeping them closed. Now imagine yourself slowly walking down a staircase of ten stairs. As you descend, silently count backwards from ten to one, with each stair representing one number. When you've reached the bottom of the stairway, imagine yourself entering a darkened screening room with many empty seats. Visualize yourself sitting down. Now project onto the screen any situation or circumstance that has recently caused you pain, or that is doing so now—anything that's bringing negative energy into your daily life and causing you to *re*act rather than *pro*act. In the imaginary film you're creating, see yourself behaving in this reactive manner. At the same time, visualize the responses of the other people in the situation. Make the scene as realistic as possible. If your attention is sufficiently well focused, the movie will almost create itself.

Once the scene has played itself out, imagine that the screen is again blank for a moment. Think about what you've just seen, and about how your behavior might have been different. What could you have done proactively instead of reactively? How could you have been different—and better—in order to make everyone else better? How could you have turned an otherwise chaotic moment into an opportunity for continuity and sharing? In short, how could you have brought the Light to this specific setting, and to yourself as a participant in it?

Now, keeping these ideas in mind, project a new movie onto the screen—one that expresses the more positive and proactive scenario. Again, if you've imagined this with clarity and attention, the scene will transpire almost effortlessly. If this doesn't happen at first, allow the screen to go blank again and start the process over. When you feel that you've visualized the best possible outcome, imagine yourself getting to your feet and slowly ascending the stairs, counting from one to ten as you do so. Finally, before you open your eyes, make a commitment to changing yourself and your responses when difficult circumstances arise. Do this very proactively. Ask the Light to present you with a challenge, and ask for help in recognizing it as an opportunity for transformation.

Colors, Numbers, and Boxes

A second visualization technique is especially useful for dealing with specific negative emotions such as envy, fear, or anger. Begin by closing your eyes, rolling them upward for a moment, and then returning your eyes to a relaxed position while still keeping them closed. Now imagine the number "3" in a bright green color against the blackness of your closed eyes. Gaze at it for a second, then replace it with the number "2" in bright blue. After a moment, replace the "2" with "1" in glistening white.

Now see the "1" dissolving into a favorite setting from your real life, somewhere you feel safe and at peace. This can be a location you visited only once, perhaps on a vacation, or it can be a place you go every day. In this secure haven, imagine that you're holding a small, sturdy box made of polished wood with a hinged lid. Imagine that any negative feeling that's troubling you is going into the box. As you do this, don't bother with realistic details such as what an emotion looks like or how it moves from one place to another. Just experience it leaving your body and your consciousness and entering the box. Then imagine yourself closing the lid.

Now that you're free of the negativity that's burdened you, ask the Creator to help you heal, so that you can be a more loving and sharing person. Feel your soul gain liberation from the pain you've been experiencing. Promise yourself to live in a way that will allow you to remain free.

Last, imagine that a beautiful beam of white light, a powerful force for healing and cleansing, descends from above to illuminate the wooden box. In your mind's eye, imagine that the box itself begins to glow. Watch this taking place for a moment and then, as the beam begins to withdraw, see yourself opening the box. It is now completely empty.

Take a deep breath and open your eyes. Gently return your consciousness to your physical setting. By performing this meditation every day, you can reduce the influence of destructive emotions and eliminate the negative consequences that arise from them.

Go into daily life

We spoke above about some steps shared by the many varieties of kabbalistic meditation—taking responsibility, for example, and making a conscious decision to connect with the Light. A final, equally useful step involves using meditation as a tool for taking positive action in the physical world. Kabbalah does not view meditation as a ride on a magic carpet. Meditation does not transport us away from the challenges of daily life. Rather, it helps us to see those challenges as occasions for growth and positive change. If we are experiencing distress, we should not and cannot "meditate" that distress away. Rather, meditation is a foundation-building step toward positive action. It brings us new strength, focus, and certainty. In turn, these help us to live our lives as truly sharing human beings.

CHAPTER 9

Sharing
the Way

In the introduction to this book, we asked some fundamental questions:

1. What is the purpose of our lives?
2. What is the meaning, if any, of human pain and suffering?
3. What are the choices that lie in our power, and what is beyond our choosing?
4. How can we find peace and satisfaction in a world that often seems chaotic and dangerous?
5. How can we make a positive difference, not only for ourselves but for others as well?

I hope *The Way* has given you some meaningful answers to those questions. In this last chapter, we will briefly review what the answers are according to kabbalistic teaching. But perhaps some clarity can also be achieved by looking at what the answers are *not*. Some years ago, the Nobel Prize–winning physicist Steven Weinberg made an extraordinary statement: "The more the universe seems comprehensible, the more it also seems pointless." This pronouncement deserves to be considered very seriously. It was made, after all, by someone who has spent his life studying nature at its most fundamental levels. But it is also the very opposite of everything Kabbalah teaches, and of everything that this book has tried to communicate.

Let me be very clear about this:

According to Kabbalah, the more we know about the universe, the more we realize how meaningful it is.

What's more, Kabbalah tells us very specifically what that meaning is. As we have said many times (but never enough), the meaning is to transform desire to receive for the self alone into desire to receive for the purpose of sharing, and to love our neighbors as ourselves.

Kabbalah's answers to the fundamental questions

1 The purpose of our life is to complete a profound spiritual transformation.

The purpose is to transform the desire to receive for ourselves alone into the desire to receive in order to share with others.

Achieving this transformation requires us to first look closely at our thoughts, our words, and our deeds, and to realize the extent to which our lives are controlled by self-serving desire. Then we must begin to remove this desire slowly, step by step, part after part. This is not an easy process. It's a process for a lifetime. But it is the only way to achieve true and lasting ful-fillment. Desire to receive for the self alone is the only thing that stands in the way of our transformation and the oneness with the Creator that it represents. This cannot be accom-plished without our actively assisting others to transform their nature as well. It may sound grandiose, but we must work to change not only ourselves but the world as a whole. We are all in the same boat. We either arrive together or we don't arrive at all.

2 Pain and suffering are present in our lives for two reasons: It may be that there has not been positive action on our part, or it may be a cleansing process to free us of negative influence.

In any case, we always have the choice to live proactively and positively, regardless of any trials we are called upon to face. This is the free will with which we are endowed by the Creator. By making proactive choices, we literally elevate ourselves above the angels into direct and active participation with God. Should we choose not to change proactively, our transformation will still come about, but it will be in response to the pain and suffering that develop directly out of our negativity and our attachment to the self-centered desire to receive.

3 Our choices make all the difference in the world.

All our actions, no matter how seemingly insignificant, influence the spiritual progress of the world. Every kindness, every moment of empathy and compassion, every act of true sharing, elevates the potential for sharing to occur somewhere in the world. Every righteous action is like the fluttering of a butterfly's wing that amplifies into a whirlwind.

4 Peace and satisfaction—real peace, real satisfaction—are the direct result of our connection to the Light of the Creator.

When we feel empty and alone, when we feel sadness, anger, or confusion, we are experiencing the absence of Light in our lives. As a result, we may find ourselves pursuing wealth, fame, or power—and we may even feel temporarily excited and fulfilled. But these flashes fade very quickly.

From the beginning of time, the Creator has had a plan for us. The apparently random nature of the events in our lives is an illusion—one imposed by a negative force whose purpose is to obscure and obstruct our connection to the Creator. But without this negative force and the choices it offers, we could not earn the fulfillment the Light contains.

5 Individual transformation is just the first step.

Kabbalah is much more than a personal self-help methodology. It is intended by the Creator not just to enrich the lives of a certain number of individuals, but to fundamentally change the nature of existence for everyone. Toward this end, we must view spreading the wisdom of Kabbalah as a highly positive action in its own right. Share these tools and teachings with as many people as possible. This will assist in your own transformation, as well as that of others.

Ultimately, when a sufficiently large number of people have achieved fulfillment through the tools of Kabbalah, a collective transformation will come about, bringing an end to the chaos and pain that have been humanity's lot since the sin of Adam. Death itself, the ultimate expression of human suffering, will vanish from the universe, and our oneness with the Creator will be complete. Remember that your spiritual work is never for yourself alone. Your smallest righteous action may be the one that creates the critical mass.

A call to action

Without taking action in the world—both for ourselves and to help others—no amount of introspection, meditation, prayer, or study will bring about spiritual transformation. Without physical action, even the most spiritual person is like a new car without an engine: it looks great, but it doesn't go anywhere.

Kabbalah is not about retreating into a lonely metaphysical

desert in order to await enlightenment. On the contrary, Kabbalah asks us to directly involve ourselves in the experience of the world as a whole, and to actively work toward healing the pain and suffering of others. Kabbalah asks us to enter wholeheartedly into life, conscious of the spiritual dangers that lie ahead, and armed with awareness of our spiritual purpose.

The key to identifying a truly transforming action is the difficulty of the act itself. By this we can understand that it is not the *quantity* of our sharing that counts, but the *quality*. Because we are creatures whose dominant characteristic is to receive for ourselves alone, one of the most difficult things we can do is to place another person's needs ahead of our own. Consequently, any action that firmly places another's needs before our own will certainly benefit in our own spiritual transformation and in the transformation of the world.

The ultimate goal of any action is the transformation of our nature—and as we transform our nature, we transform the world.

Opportunities for transforming action present themselves at every turn. In fact, these opportunities are not only right outside the front door, they are very often right inside our living room. For example, becoming a less judgmental and more loving parent and spouse may be more transforming than donating thousands of dollars to a charitable organization—because for some of us it is more difficult to open our hearts to our own families than to open our checkbook to strangers.

It is for this reason that the wisdom of Kabbalah suggests that we turn our attention to that which is difficult for us to do.

It is a spiritual law that where there is the most potential for spiritual transformation, *that* is where the desire to receive for the self alone, will resist with its greatest force. Fear, self-doubt, pride, even sadness may rise up to convince us of the impossibility of our endeavors. Each is a manifestation of the desire to receive for the self alone, and each represents a sign of our negativity resisting change. The difficulties themselves are merely signs of the spiritual potential of our journey. When the road gets tough, remember that this road can lead us beyond all pain, sorrow, and self-doubt to a destination of fulfillment beyond anything we have ever known.

The Light of the Creator is revealed to a person depending on how much he believes and knows that the Light will be revealed. If a person does an action that has the ability to draw to him the Light of the Creator, that is still is not enough. He needs to *believe* that this action has the ability to draw to him the Light of the Creator. Remember: the amount of Light revealed through his action accords exactly with his understanding of his power. The more we understand and believe in our ability to draw the Light of the Creator, the more Light we will draw.

The following story is said to have taken place several hundred years ago, somewhere in Eastern Europe. The events described in the narrative may not be completely factually accurate, but in the most important respects I believe that this story is as true as any that has ever been told.

The Envelopes Slipped under the Doors

A traveler was passing on the outskirts of a town when he noticed a newly dug grave in the middle of an open field. At the head of the grave there was a simple marker made of wood. It read: "HERE LIES YOSSELE."

"That's strange," thought the traveler. "Why has this man been buried out here in the fields? Why wasn't he given a decent burial in the cemetery?"

When the traveler entered the town a short time later, he sought out the local rabbi and inquired about the lonely grave he'd seen. "How did such a thing come to be?" he asked the rabbi. "Why wasn't this Yossele buried in the cemetery with everyone else?"

The rabbi shook his head and shrugged. "Truthfully, he was lucky to be buried at all. Actually, I put him in the ground all by myself. No one would bury him, let alone mourn for him. You see, Yossele was the stingiest person who ever lived. Even when he knew he was about to pass on and our burial society asked him to pay the fee for his funeral, he simply refused. Can you imagine that? Yossele had only a few days to live and he couldn't stand to part with the money to pay for his own funeral!"

"That's amazing," said the traveler. "So you buried him yourself?"

"Yes," said the rabbi.

"Well, you did a noble thing, then, even if this Yossele didn't deserve it."

The rabbi bowed his head—and just at that moment there was a knock on the front door. "Excuse me," said the rabbi to the traveler. He opened the door, and there stood what was obviously a very poor man. He was dressed in rags, but that was not the worst of it. He looked extremely worried.

"What can I do for you?" asked the rabbi.

The poor man sounded desperate. "I just need a little money in order to buy something to eat."

The rabbi nodded, and took some money from his pocket for the man. Then he closed the door and returned his attention to the traveler. But just as they were resuming their conversation there was another knock on the door. Excusing himself once again, the rabbi opened the door and found himself confronted by a second impoverished man.

"What can I do for you?" asked the rabbi.

"Please," said the man. "I need some money for food."

Reaching into his pocket once again, the rabbi gave the man some money and shut the door. Then he turned back to the traveler, and they picked up their talk where it had left off. But just then there was yet a third knock on the door. And when the rabbi opened it, another poor man stood before him. What's more, as he looked over this man's shoulder the rabbi could see even more poor people making their way toward his house. There was a whole crowd of them.

"What's going on here?" said the rabbi. "I never even knew there were this many impoverished people in the whole town!" He looked at the man in the doorway. "How has this happened? Where have you all been hiding? And why are you so suddenly coming to me now?"

The poor man replied with a note of desperation in his voice, "No one needed help until now. For years there was someone who took care of all the poor people in the area. Somehow, between midnight and dawn every Wednesday, an envelope with enough money for the week would appear under the doors of our homes. But now Wednesday has come and gone and there have been no envelopes. What are we going to do?"

As the rabbi searched his home for enough money to distribute to the many people outside, he wondered aloud to the traveler about an explanation for this mystery. But the traveler was indeed a traveler in the deepest sense of the term. He was a man of the world.

As the rabbi continued to pass out coins, the traveler spoke up. "By the way, when was it exactly that Yossele died?"

"It was last Thursday," said the rabbi.

"And today is Thursday again. So the end of the envelopes corresponds with the death of the miser."

Now both the rabbi and the poor people gathered at the door looked at the traveler in disbelief. "You're not suggesting that Yossele was the one who was giving away the money, are you?"

"Well," said the traveler, "I don't see what other explanation there could be. This is not a village where a lot of people come and go. No one else has passed on. It must be him."

The rabbi's eyes widened—first in amazement, and then in realization of the truth. Yossele had been a miser, but a holy miser. Everyone had been wrong about him, and that was the way he had wanted it. He had kept the truth to himself with the same determination that he'd seemed to use in holding onto his money!

That very day the rabbi saw to it that the town's whole population gathered to mourn Yossele's passing, and to pray for his forgiveness. They stood together—all the people who had thought Yossele was beneath their contempt, and who now looked up to him as a truly righteous person—the more so since he had kept his virtue a secret.

But then yet another completely unexpected event took place. As the rabbi was eulogizing Yossele as the holy miser, he suddenly felt himself losing touch with the physical world. Yet it

wasn't as if he were sick or dying, or even just losing consciousness. Instead, it was like a state of heightened awareness.

The rabbi was having a vision. He was standing alone with
Yossele somewhere high above the earth. "Yossele," he said, "I'm
so sorry about the way you were treated when you were alive. We
just didn't know."

"Of course not," said Yossele kindly. "I didn't want you to
know. It wasn't for the purpose of obtaining anything, and certainly not recognition. It was for giving, not getting."

"But still," said the rabbi, "it must be very gratifying for you
now in the celestial realms. There, I'm certain, you consort with
the great patriarchs and matriarchs—with Abraham, Isaac, Jacob,
Moses, and David . . . with Sarah and Leah and Rachel and
Rebecca."

The very mention of these sacred names sent a chill down the
rabbi's back. But he was surprised to see a somewhat distant look
on the face of Yossele.

"Isn't being in the presence of those great souls the supreme
achievement of creation?" the rabbi asked. "Isn't it the most a
soul can ever hope to attain?"

"Yes, it's very wonderful," agreed Yossele. "But—"

"But?" said the rabbi expectantly. "But?"

And now Yossele spoke with sudden conviction: "But nothing—not even being in the presence of the Creator—can compare
with slipping those envelopes under the doors on Wednesday
nights."

I love this story for its teaching that ultimate fulfillment
depends on our passage into another dimension of existence.

Fulfillment is yours when you become a being of sharing, and when you perform the acts of sharing that naturally flow from this.

As I write these final lines of *The Way*, I'm very much aware of the great opportunity that exists in our lives:

Fulfillment awaits us—right here, right now.

And I'm also aware of the imminent need to take advantage of this opportunity. In the Introduction, I discussed the fear I'd felt at the prospect that I would someday have to say good-bye to my parents if they left this world. I suggested that you, too, had undoubtedly experienced something like this fear, and I assured you that the tools of Kabbalah could help you bring an end to that.

The Way has given me the means to present those tools, and writing it at this point in my life has made their importance clearer than ever. I'm now a husband and a father. There are more people to whom I never want to say good-bye, more people whom I deeply wish to see liberated from any form of suffering. I know there are many such people in your life also.

I hope you will now begin using the sacred tools of Kabbalah to hasten your own transformation, and that you will pass on these tools to others, so that together we can achieve the end of pain, suffering, and death for all mankind—so that together we can live in the Light and experience fulfillment.

Glossary

akideh   (lit., binding) This refers to the episode described in Genesis 22, when the Creator called upon Abraham to offer his son, Isaac, as a sacrifice. Here, Kabbalah explains, Isaac's spiritual nature of *gevurah* (judgment) was mitigated or "sweetened" by Abraham's essence of *chesed* (kindness, mercy).

Bat Kol   (lit., a voice [from above]) The kabbalists explain that each of us experiences this moment of inner spiritual awakening. *Bat Kol* is a sudden flash of the Creator's Light.

chesed   Kindness. One of the ten *sefirot*.

d'vekut   (lit., bonding) Kabbalah teaches that the ultimate purpose of our spiritual work is the supreme fulfillment that comes when *d'vekut* with the Creator is achieved.

ein sof   (lit., endless) The kabbalists use this term to refer to the Creator. Although we cannot comprehend the Creator's nature, His endlessness is one attribute we can grasp.

Elohim   A name of God. The Creator has many names, each of which denotes one of His emanations. Each name expresses a different manifestation of the Creator's Light.

emunah   (lit., trust [in the creator]) This is not blind faith. *Emunah* is trust built on understanding of the Creator's love, and of the power of the kabbalistic tools that the Creator has provided for us.

gevurah   (lit., might) One of the ten *sefirot*. *Gevurah* expresses the energy of judgment.

Kabbalah   The ancient wistom given by the Creator to all mankind; the path set forth by God to bring about fulfillment and to remove pain, suffering, and even death from the world.

kavanah   (lit., intention, especially with regard to thought) *Kavanah* is an important element of kabbalistic meditation, which often includes focused attention (as on a combination of Hebrew letters) in order to direct and draw a specific flow of Light.

Light of the Creator   We cannot comprehend the Creator, but we interact and connect to His Light, which is the source of all joy and fulfillment.

malchut   (lit., kingdom) The last of ten *sefirot*. *Malchut* manifests the Light of the Creator. It is the Vessel to which the Light flows.

nahama dichisufa   "Bread of shame." Kabbalah teaches that we must earn the Light, not simply receive it. Our essential nature is that of the Creator. Like Him, we cannot accept "free gifts." We have come to this world to earn the Light, and when this is achieved we are set free of the "bread of shame."

Sefer Yetzirah   *The Book of Formation.* The kabbalists attribute this book to Abraham the Patriarch. It is a fascinating revelation of the creation of the world by the Hebrew alphabet, with an explanation of each letter's spiritual power.

Shabbat   The Sabbath. On the seventh day of the week, the gates of heaven are open. The Creator gives us this gift to restore our souls and to give us a glimpse of true fulfillment.

sefirah (pl. *sefirot*)   The emanations of the Creator; the spiritual channels through which His Light flows to us.

tikkun   (lit., correction) The process of spiritual mending. Each of us came to this world for the purpose of accomplishing a specific *tikkun*.

tsimtsum   (lit., constriction, or restriction) One of the first events that occurred in the primordial spiritual world. The Vessel restricted the flow of the Creator's Light in order to earn it back, rather than simply receive it.

tzaddik (pl. *tzaddikim*)   A righteous person. Kabbalah teaches that *tzaddikkim* are channels through whom we can draw Light.

tzedaka   Charity. An important spiritual act of sharing.

Vessel   The spiritual receiver. We are all Vessels for the Light of the Creator. As Vessels, we manifest the Light.

Zohar   The source of kabbalistic knowledge revealed by Rabbi Shimon bar Yochai two thousand years ago. By reading the Zohar—or even just scanning it—we draw great Light to ourselves and the world.

Bibliography and Sources for Further Reading

Ashlag, Rabbi Yehuda. *An Entrance to the Zohar.* Dr. Philip S. Berg, ed. The Research Centre of Kabbalah. New York and Jerusalem, 1974.

———. *Kabbalah: A Gift of the Bible.* The Research Centre of Kabbalah. New York and Jerusalem, 1984.

Rav Berg. *Education of a Kabbalist.* New York and Los Angeles: The Kabbalah Centre, 2000.

Berg, Rabbi Philip S. *A Study of the Ten Luminous Emanations from Rabbi Isaac Luria.* The Research Centre of Kabbalah. New York and Jerusalem, 1973.

———. *Wheels of a Soul.* New York and Los Angeles: The Kabbalah Centre, 2000.

Kaplan, Aryeh, ed. *Sefer Yetzirah: The Book of Creation.* York Beach, Maine. Samuel Weiser, Inc. 1997.

Kaplan, Aryeh, trans. *The Bahir.* York Beach, Maine. Samuel Weiser Inc., 1990.

Luzzatto, Rabbi Moshe Chaim. *The Path of the Just.* Jerusalem and New York. Feldheim Publishers, 1993.

———. *The Way of God.* Jerusalem and New York. Feldheim Publishers, 1983.

bar Yochai, Rabbi Shimon. *The Zohar.* Tel Aviv and New York: The Press of Yeshivat Kol Yehuda.

Index

"bread of shame," 58–59
breathing meditation, 211–13
butterfly effect, 100, 229

Abraham the Patriarch, 25, 49, 50, 164,
    187, 196–98, 203
actions
    and angels, 101–102
    charity, 158
    helping others, 73, 130–31, 132, 230–31
    and joy, 136–37
    and meditation, 225
    and miracles, 192
    negative, 79–82, 94–95, 121, 157
    repentance for, 121–22
    results of, 100–101, 157, 229
    significance of, 6, 88–89, 94, 100–103,
        130, 213, 229–32
    and spiritual growth, 63, 156–57
    and suffering, 228
    and testing, 119–21
    and trust, 116
    and Upper Worlds, 57
Adam and Eve, 24–25, 63, 165
Akiva, Rabbi, 77–79
angels, 101–102
anger, 144–45, 217, 223
appreciation, 137–39
Ari. *See* Luria, Isaac
"As above, so below" principle, 57, 216
Ashlag, Yehuda, 31, 50, 90, 126, 193. 194
awe, 144

Baal Shem Tov, 30–31, 82, 84–85, 96,
    169–71, 175
bar Yochai, Shimon, 28, 185
Bat Kol, 110–11
ben Eliezer, Israel. *See* Baal Shem Tov
Berg, Karen and Rav, 31
Berlin, Naftali Zvi Yehuda, 20–22
Bible, meditating on, 213–14
Big Bang theory, 41–42
blessing, Shabbat, 184–85
blindness, spiritual, 127–28
Book of Formation, The, 26
Book of Splendor, 28–32
Brandwein, Yehuda, 31

cause and effect, laws of, 80–81
chaos theory, 100
charity, 157–65, 183
chesed, 197
children, and Shabbat, 184–85
choices, importance of, 71, 80–82, 96, 229
coincidences, 111–12, 191
colors, numbers, and boxes meditation,
    223–25
complacency, 124–27
concentration, in prayer, 175
consciousness, nature of, 42
Cordovero, Moses, 29
creation, purpose of, 39
creation story, 35–42, 52
Creator. *See also* Light of the Creator
    and Adam and Eve, 24–25
    attributes of, 15–16, 39, 58
    conversations with, 214–16
    disconnection from, 44, 45–46, 65, 80,
        95, 145
    help from, 89–92, 116–17
    intentions of, 17–18, 20, 39, 40, 126, 229
    judgment of, 96–100
    and meditation, 214–16
    Oneness with, 16, 42, 57, 60, 65, 158,
        216, 217, 230
    and prayer, 166–68, 173–74
    relationship with, 79, 92, 167–68, 199
    and study, 196–98, 199
    trust in, 112–16, 139–40
    wisdom of, 33
Cubs, 29

death
    death of, 53, 56, 129, 230
    kabbalistic understanding of, 4, 7, 53,
        56
    motivating power of, 128–29
    near-death experiences, 128–29
deeds. *See* actions
desire, self-serving. *See* self-serving desire
divine assistance, 116–17

241